Finding the Magic

Emergent Readers and Writers

Melinda Miller

Sam Houston State University

Kendall Hunt
publishing company

Cover image © Shutterstock.com

www.kendallhunt.com
Send all inquiries to:
4050 Westmark Drive
Dubuque, IA 52004-1840

Copyright © 2020 by Kendall Hunt Publishing Company

ISBN 978-1-7924-2179-2

All rights reserved. No part of this publication may be reproduced,
stored in a retrieval system, or transmitted, in any form or by any means,
electronic, mechanical, photocopying, recording, or otherwise,
without the prior written permission of the copyright owner.

Published in the United States of America

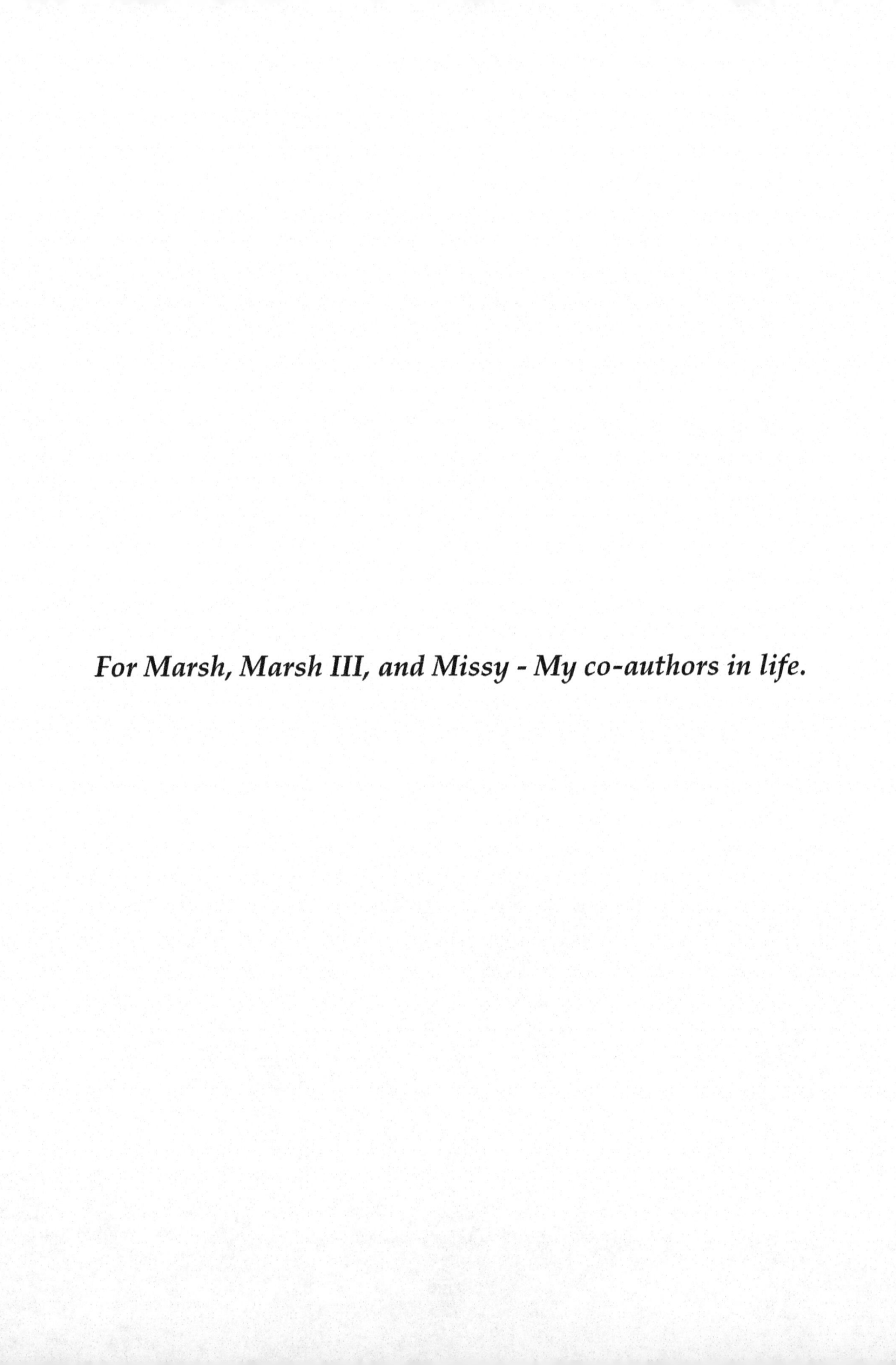

For Marsh, Marsh III, and Missy - My co-authors in life.

CONTENTS

Chapter 1 **Literacy Learning Theories and Stages** 1
  Constructivism 3
  Piaget 3
  Vygotsky 4
  Transactional Theory 6
  Bandura 7
  Literacy Stages 7
  Spelling Stages 10
  Balanced Literacy Approach 12

Chapter 2 **Learning to Read** 15
  The Beginnings 16
  Cueing Systems 17
  Scaffolding 17
  Read-Aloud 18
  Shared Reading 19
  Guided Reading 21
  Reading Strategies 24
  Independent Reading 26

Chapter 3 **Learning to Write** 31
  The Beginnings 32
  Write-Aloud 33
  Shared Writing 35
  Independent Writing 37

Chapter 4 Reading and Writing in the Classroom 43

Phonics 44

Word Work 48

Hearing and Recording Sounds in Words 48

Making and Breaking Words 49

Analogies 49

Chunks 50

My Pile/Your Pile 50

Vocabulary 52

Fluency 54

Comprehension 56

Literacy Centers 57

Chapter 5 Reading Workshop 61

Reading Mini-Lessons 63

Independent Reading Time 64

Responding to Text 65

Conferences 67

Sharing Time 68

Finding the Right Book 69

Chapter 6 Writing Workshop 73

Writing Mini-Lessons 75

Status of the Class 75

Independent Writing Time 76

Writer's Craft 81

Writing Conferences 82

Sharing Writing 84

Chapter 7 Literature for Young Readers 87

The Importance of Choice 87

Predictable Books 89

Big Books   90

Alphabet Books   91

Word Play Books   92

Concept Books   93

Wordless Picture Books   94

Multicultural Books   94

Critical Literacy   95

Acquiring Books   98

Motivating Readers   98

Chapter 8   The Multicultural Classroom   105

Including all Cultures   106

English Learners   114

Accepting Home Languages   118

Including Families   120

Chapter 9   Assessing Reading and Writing   125

Ongoing Informal Assessment   125

Informal Reading Inventory   128

Running Records   129

Spelling Inventories   131

Observations and Anecdotal Records   131

Rubrics   132

Reading and Writing Conferences   133

Work Samples   135

Portfolios   135

Self-Assessment   136

Parent Conferences   137

High-Stakes Tests   138

Chapter 10 Loving School 143

Creating a Community 145

Focusing on the Positive 147

Using Music in the Classroom 150

Combining Art and Literature 153

Slowing Down 153

Finding Magic in the Classroom 154

CHAPTER 1

Literacy Learning Theories and Stages

Ms. Lee is excited to begin a new school year. This is her seventh year to teach, but her first year to teach first grade. She has been teaching second grade for the last 6 years and feels confident using Reading and Writing Workshops along with read-aloud, shared reading, guided reading, write-aloud, shared writing, and mini-lessons. She knows how important the workshop model is for meeting individual needs and for giving students time to orchestrate all they know about reading and writing during independent reading and writing time. On the first day of school, Ms. Lee's new first graders excitedly arrive one by one with their moms, dads, grandparents, or siblings. They have already met their new teacher at Meet the Teacher night, and they are happy to see her again as she shows them to their seats. There are markers, different colors of paper, books, playdough, and magnetic letters at each table for the students to explore while all the other children arrive. The day will be a busy one, as students learn about their new classroom, listen to stories, and play name games. The first few weeks will be all about creating a community of learners, reading and writing every day, and learning all about each other. As Ms. Lee gets to know her first graders, she gives them the Observation Survey and the Spelling Inventory and realizes her students are on many different levels. One child, Andres, can read Little House on the Prairie books, two other children are learning to spell their names and can write a few letters, while other students fall everywhere in between. Ms. Lee smiles to herself because she knows exactly what to do. She will think about the learning theories and base her instruction on what she knows are best practices. She will again use Reading and Writing

Workshops and she will cater her instruction to meet individual needs. She will use read-aloud and write-aloud to model the reading and writing processes. Then she will guide students through reading and writing with guided reading and shared writing. She will design her mini-lessons based upon what she sees in her students' reading and writing, and she will give them word work to help them learn all about words and how they work. She will provide plenty of uninterrupted time every day for students to actually read and write independently on their own levels with reading and writing materials of their choice. She will conference with her students to monitor their progress and provide individual instruction. Students will be able to respond to what they have read through extension activities and publish their writing pieces. Finally, Ms. Lee will invite students to share what they have read and written with the class, and she and other students will respond back to them with questions and ideas. She knows that she will be able to build a community of readers and writers who support one another in their literacy development. She knows she will be able to support all students through scaffolding, recognize and celebrate the cultures of all students, and make all students feel they belong to and are valued by the community in the classroom. Ms. Lee will do everything she can to make sure each and every student will have the best possible year they can have, and that they will find joy and magic in the classroom they all share.

When we think about literacy learning, we must remember that all children learn differently and at different rates. The most important thing to remember is to create a print-rich environment where all students can work at their own levels and at their own pace in order to become proficient readers and writers. There are several different theories we must remember as we think about what is best for our students. A description of several theories follows, so that you might discover what is best for your students.

Constructivism

The Constructivist theory states that children construct their own learning through integrating their prior experiences with new knowledge (Tompkins, 2015). Learners base new knowledge on what they already know, and "move from the known to the new" (Templeton, 1995, p. 12). According to Tompkins, "This theory is child centered because teachers engage children with experiences so that they can construct their own knowledge" (p. 7). In addition, constructivists believe that "Learning is rooted in the relationship between actions, context, and culture" (Lasley, Haas, & Nabors, 2016, p. 162).

Piaget

Jean Piaget (1969) was a constructivist and theorized that "Children take an active role in the construction of their knowledge through experiences with their world" (Lasley et al., 2016, p. 164). Piaget described how learning is organized through schema. Schema can be thought of as a filing system, and every experience a child has is filed away in their brain. As children learn new things, either they go into an existing file because they relate to prior knowledge, or when a child learns something new, their brain makes a new file to put it in. Every new thing we learn is placed into a file of similar knowledge to which we make connections. Assimilation occurs when the topic can be connected to familiar material. Sometimes we see something or read something that does not fit into our schema. In that case, our schema is modified as we interact with our prior knowledge, our lived experiences, and our environment, and we learn something new as our brain creates a new file through accommodation (Tompkins, 2015). Piaget's schema theory is important to keep in mind as we teach children. We need to always remember to keep the students' prior

knowledge in mind and help them make connections to the familiar. As they are learning new things, we must build their background knowledge and provide a context for them that gives them the support they will need to construct their own learning.

Vygotsky

Sociolinguistics is a theory that "Learners use language to organize their thoughts" (Tompkins, 2014, p. 8). Lev Vygotsky, a sociolinguist (1978), theorized that learning is social and that language and thinking go together to help us learn. For this reason, it is important to incorporate conversation among our students as part of their learning, so students can talk about and process what they are learning with their peers (Tompkins, 2015). Especially, English learners should have many opportunities to practice using their new language throughout the day (Seidlitz, 2019).

Vygotsky also coined the term, zone of proximal development (ZPD), to describe the place between what a child is able to do on their own and what they can do with assistance from an adult or a more knowledgeable peer. The ZPD "includes all of the knowledge and skills that children cannot yet understand or perform on their own yet are capable of learning with guidance" (Lasley et al., 2016, p. 173). The teacher starts with heavy support and gradually removes the support as the child becomes more and more independent. Eventually, the child will do the task on their own. For example, a teacher can choose a book that is slightly above a child's reading level, then give a detailed book introduction, and prompt the child as they are reading. The child is able to read the book with few miscues with a combination of their sight word knowledge, their understanding of text, and support from the teacher.

According to Vygotsky, "What a child can do in cooperation today, he can do alone tomorrow" (Vygotsky, p.). Scaffolding provided by a teacher gives students the support they need to become independent. In the beginning, the teacher gives heavy support, then gradually withdraws support as the child becomes more independent. According to Seidlitz (2019), "In the context of language development, scaffolding provides specific targeted support so that students gradually become self-sufficient in their language production" (p. 40). Seidlitz emphasizes that English learners need scaffolding from their teachers to become independent in reading, writing, listening, and speaking. Three types of scaffolding are oral scaffolding, procedural scaffolding, and instructional scaffolding. In oral scaffolding, teachers use a lot of modeling, and they rephrase language without direct correcting. Procedural scaffolding involves moving from whole group to small group or partner work, and eventually to individual work. For example, a teacher might start out with a write-aloud, move into an interactive writing activity, then ask students to write on their own. Through instructional scaffolding, teachers provide graphic organizers, think-alouds, and sentence stems to support students as they learn (Echevarria, Vogt, & Short, 2017; Seidlitz, 2019).

Another theory that fits under the umbrella of Sociolinguistics is Sociocultural theory. According to Tompkins (2014), in this theory, "Reading and writing are viewed as social activities that reflect the culture and community in which the students live, and students from different cultures have different expectations about literacy learning and preferred ways of learning" (p. 9). Teachers can create classroom environments that take Sociocultural theory into consideration by ensuring all cultures are recognized and celebrated and by using culturally responsive teaching. Within this type of classroom environment, teachers make a concerted effort to include all students' cultures within lessons, class decorations, and literature. Chapter 7 discusses using multicultural literature and critical literature, and Chapter 8 talks about the multicultural classroom.

Transactional Theory

Louise Rosenblatt (1978) states that students construct meaning as they read a text. According to Rosenblatt (2013), a transaction occurs between the author, the text, and the reader when one reads a text. Each reading of a text is unique, and readers bring their background knowledge and lived experiences to a text when they read. Tompkins (2014) states that "Instead of trying to figure out the author's meaning, readers negotiate an interpretation based on the text and their knowledge about literature and the world" (p. 12). You can think of it as a piece of art. Everyone brings different experiences to that piece of art and will interpret it in a different way. As students read a text, we must keep this in mind. Students interpret texts differently because of their lived experiences. As Tompkins puts it, "Even though interpretations vary, they can always be substantiated by the text" (p. 12).

Templeton and Gehsmann (2014) tell us that "When children respond to a text, they are interpreting it" (p. 287). In Rosenblatt's (1978) Transactional model, readers have a response to what they read that is an efferent stance, in which the focus is on learning something or acquiring information; or an aesthetic stance, which is a personal connection and has to do with enjoyment or appreciation of the text. The response can also be anywhere between these two stances. According to Templeton and Gehsmann, purpose for reading is important in regard to a reader's stance. They state, "Prior knowledge, critical thinking skills, motivation, engagement, and thoughtful reasoning all come into play when the reader transacts with a text" (p. 287). A reader's response can also be efferent and aesthetic at the same time, and it is common to have new responses when a text is reread. I have read *Number the Stars* (Lowery, 1989) to my college reading classes several times. Each time I read, it is different and more powerful to me. I have an emotional response to the book, and it becomes more intense with each reading. Knowing how the story ends can cause you to read the whole text differently.

Bandura

Learners who are engaged in the reading process are more confident in their reading ability, especially when they are reading text that they are interested in (Bandura, 1997). According to Tompkins, "Children with high self-efficacy are resilient and persistent despite the obstacles that get in the way of their success" (Tompkins, 2015, p. 8). ". . . if the child believes he or she can complete a task that is difficult, he or she will engage in the task and remain engaged for a much longer time than a child who enters the task with expectations of failure" (Lasley et al., 2016, p. 117). Students must participate in authentic, engaging literacy activities in order to be successful in the literacy classroom, and they must have a choice of what to read and write.

Literacy Stages

All children learn and develop differently and at different rates. We can use literacy stages to determine approximately where a child should be at a given age, though there is a lot of variation among children. It is best to think of a child as an individual and meet them where they are developmentally, using the literacy stages as a guideline. There are many different names given to literacy stages, depending upon the researcher describing them. The following literacy stages come from Cooper (2000).

Early Emergent Literacy In the Early Emergent stage, children begin to develop a foundation of literacy, and they begin to develop oral language. The child is curious about print, and writing is done by drawing or scribbling. The child knows the concept of a book and that print has purpose. This stage usually occurs before the child enters Kindergarten. Children may engage in pretend reading, or they may read a book for memory. When they write something down, they may use scribbles at first, then a combination of drawings and letters. In my Kindergarten class, most of the students told their stories through scribbles and pictures until about January, when they began to use letters with their drawings.

Emergent Literacy In the Emergent Literacy stage, the child becomes more interested in literacy and uses more conventional oral language. The child develops concepts about print and is able to form and name letters. Usually, this stage is completed by the end of Kindergarten or the beginning of first grade. I have a distinct memory from when I was learning to read. I was reading aloud to my mom in a dentist's office waiting room, and was pointing to words as I went. Two younger girls were watching me read, and they pretended to read magazines. I knew they couldn't read because they turned the pages so quickly and didn't look at the print, but I did notice they were turning pages from the front of the book to the back, so they did have some concepts about print.

Beginning Reading and Writing   In the Beginning Reading and Writing stage, children begin to read and write in conventional ways. They are able to decode words and start to develop fluency in reading. Their vocabulary knowledge increases. This stage is typical of first graders and sometimes second and third graders. I have talked with many other first grade teachers about the "magic moment" when first graders begin to read conventionally. It is as if they go home one day as an emergent reader, and come back the next day reading! Reading suddenly clicks for them, and they just take off!

Almost Fluent Reading and Writing   In the Almost Fluent Reading and Writing stage, the child's literacy becomes more sophisticated. The child reads mostly silently, writes more, and has a larger oral vocabulary. Students are able to use word recognition strategies and are better able to construct meaning. This stage typically lasts from second grade until fourth or fifth grade. Every year, there was a time in my second grade class when students were suddenly reading chapter books and writing long and involved pieces. That was magic, too!

Fluent Reading and Writing   In the Fluent Reading and Writing stage, the student uses reading, writing, and oral language for a variety of purposes and has acquired most literacy skills. Word recognition is well developed and a wide variety of strategies are used to get meaning. This stage begins as early as fourth grade for some students and continues throughout one's life. I have actually known two students who entered this stage in Kindergarten and first grade. They could read anything that was put in front of them and write like the wind! These were definitely two exceptions to the rule, but are examples of how all students go through stages at different times.

   Reading and writing develop together. They support each other and cannot be separated. When we think about writing development, we look at the ways students begin to listen to sounds and record them at first as drawings, then as letter-like forms, and finally as letters. Bear, Invernizzi, Templeton, and Johnston (2004) have developed the stages of spelling that can give us further information about our students' literacy development.

Spelling Stages

Emergent Spellers   The Emergent speller stage includes any child not yet reading conventionally. The typical emergent speller is newborn to age 5, but in many cases first graders or even second graders may be in this stage. Children in the Early Emergent stage go from scribble writing to drawings and random letters that do not match the sounds of the intended message. They are able to hold a crayon or pencil and write on a page. My daughter, Missy was in this stage at a year old, and she made a series of vertical marks with a pencil that she held with her fist. I was in graduate school at the time, and she saw me read my books and write annotations while I read. She also got one of my textbooks and made the same vertical marks on some of the pages of my book.

Children in the Middle Emergent stage are able to move from left to right on the page, as they make letterlike forms, and lines and dots. By this time, there is "a clear distinction between writing and drawing" (Bear et al., p. 11). By the Late Emergent stage, there is some letter sound correspondence. For example, I had a first grade student named Carlos who wrote a story about jumping on the trampoline, and he wrote "J" for "jump" and "P" for "trampoline." Children at this stage often say their

stories out loud as they are writing them. I can remember my son, Marsh, working on a Christmas tree coloring sheet in his pre-K classroom while I was helping set up for the class Christmas party. I stopped by to check on him, and I could hear him talking before I even got close to him. He was telling a story about putting lights on a Christmas tree and how they were all attached and where they plugged into the wall. He had mostly drawings of Christmas lights and a cord, and also the letters "K" and "L."

Letter Name—Alphabetic Spelling The Letter Name—Alphabetic Spelling stage usually lasts from Kindergarten until about the middle of second grade. Students in this stage use the names of letters along with the sounds of letters, and they use the alphabetical principle, that you move from left to right and put sounds and letters together to spell and read. Students in this stage have a good understanding of directionality. At the beginning of the stage, they may use two consonants to represent a word, such as "RD" for "red," or they may use the name of a letter to represent a word by the way it sounds, such as "R" for "are." By the end of the stage, the approximations students make are more similar to conventional spelling, but they may lack blends and digraphs. For example, they might write "GOT" for "goat." They are hearing the sounds and recording them as letters, for the most part, but they are not yet aware of consonant and vowel combinations.

Within Word Pattern Spelling In the Within Word Pattern stage, students are able to read with automaticity, and they may know up to 400 sight words. They are now able to spell and read many words with consonant digraphs and blends. According to Bear et al. (2004), "Since these basic phonics features have been mastered, within word pattern spellers work with the orthography and the writing system at a more abstract level than letter-name alphabetic spellers can" (p. 15). Students at this stage may even begin to understand some Latin suffixes.

The last two stages are The Syllables and Affixes Spelling stage, which begins at approximately ages 9 to 14; and the Derivational Relations stage, which normally occurs anywhere from middle school to high school. Students at these levels are able to understand vowel and consonant patterns, as well as prefixes and suffixes. They begin to understand morphology and spelling patterns. According to Bear et al. (2004), "Throughout this stage students learn about the history of words and their derivations" (p. 19). The authors also emphasize that at these stages, students' vocabularies continue to expand.

It is important to remember learning theories and literacy stages as you are making plans for your classroom and planning instruction. Tompkins states, "Understanding how children learn influences how teachers teach" (p. 6). The theories I have presented are child centered, and "advocate children's active engagement in authentic literacy activities" (p. 6). Throughout the text, you will see examples of how to teach in an interactive language-rich culturally responsive environment in a balanced literacy classroom.

Balanced Literacy Approach

A balanced literacy approach combines explicit reading and writing instruction with collaborative group work and independent reading and writing practice (Tompkins, 2014). Cooper (2000) states, "It is important we understand the necessity of a balanced program in which students have opportunities for both discovery and direct instruction" (p. 25). A balanced literacy classroom is child centered and includes scaffolded reading and writing instruction. You typically see read-aloud, shared reading, guided reading, and independent reading, as well as write-aloud, shared writing, and independent writing in a balanced literacy classroom. In addition, teachers explicitly teach skills, strategies, and procedures through mini-lessons. Students read and write through authentic literacy experiences, and teacher and students become a community of learners that accepts and celebrates all cultures. Templeton and Gehsmann (2014) stress that social and cultural contexts are important aspects of our students' literacy learning and should be a focus as we plan instruction to meet our students' needs. The attitude in the balanced literacy classroom is to meet children where they are and focus on their strengths with the goal of trying everything until we find what works to help each and every child succeed.

References

Bandura, A. (1997). *Self-efficacy: The exercise of control.* New York: W. H. Freeman.

Bear, D., Invernizzi, M., Templeton, S., & Johnston, F. (2004). *Words their way: Word study for phonics, vocabulary, and spelling instruction.* Upper Saddle River, NJ: Pearson Merrill Prentice Hall.

Cooper, J. D. (2000). *Literacy: Helping children construct meaning.* Boston, MA: Houghton Mifflin Harcourt.

Echevarria, J., Vogt, M., & Short, D. (2017). *Making content comprehensible for English learners: The SIOP Model* (5th ed.). New York: Pearson.

Lasley, E., Haas, L., & Nabors, D. (2016). *Learning through play: Early Childhood theory, development, exploration and engagement.* Dubuque, IA: Kendall Hunt Publishing Company.

Piaget, J. (1969). *The psychology of intelligence.* Paterson, NJ: Littlefield, Adams.

Rosenblatt, L. (1978). *The reader, the text, the poem: The transactional theory of the literary work.* Carbondale, IL: Southern Illinois University Press.

Rosenblatt, L. M. (2013). The transactional theory of reading and writing. In D. E. Alvermann, N. J. Unrau, & R. B. Rudell (Eds.), *Theoretical models and processes of reading* (6th ed., pp. 923–956). Newark, DE: International Reading Association.

Seidlitz, J. (2019). *Sheltered instruction in Texas: Second language acquisition methods for teachers of ELs.* Irving, TX: Seidlitz Education.

Templeton, S. (1995). *Children's literacy: Contexts for meaningful learning.* Boston, MA: Houghton Mifflin Company.

Templeton, S., & Gehsmann, K. (2014). *Teaching reading and writing: The developmental approach.* Boston, MA: Pearson.

Tompkins, G. (2014). *Literacy for the 21st century: A balanced approach.* Boston, MA: Pearson.

Tompkins, G. (2015). *Literacy in the early grades: A successful start for PreK-4 readers and writers.* Boston, MA: Pearson.

Vygotsky, L. (1978). *Mind in society.* Cambridge, MA: Harvard University Press.

CHAPTER 2

Learning to Read

In Ms. Swann's first grade classroom, a busy hum can be heard as students eagerly choose books from the book center to read for independent reading time. As they choose their books, they scatter about the classroom and sprawl with pillows and books and settle down to read. The children read quietly to themselves, or they pair up to read quietly. Ms. Swann strolls around and conferences with a few students. After about 20 minutes, she rings a bell and calls the students to the carpet for read-aloud time. She reads <u>The Day Jimmy's Boa Ate the Wash</u> (Noble, 1980) aloud to the students as they listen eagerly to find out what happens in the story. They ask questions, and sometimes stand up to point to pictures or words in the book. After they finish the book, they talk together about the funny field trip the characters in the book went on. Next, Ms. Swann calls individual groups for guided reading. She meets with two groups today and will meet with the remaining two groups the next day. While she is meeting with the groups, other students participate in literacy centers, or they read to themselves or to a partner. Finally, at the end of reading time, Ms. Swann conducts a shared reading with a big book with the whole class. She introduces <u>Where the Wild Things Are</u> (1964), turning the pages, showing the pictures, and asking the children to predict what might happen in the book. Then, she begins to read fluently and asks the children to read along. Children read along at their own level. When they get to the end of the book, they do a retelling as a class, and she takes dictation on the dry erase board as children retell the story. Next, Ms. Swann points out that each sentence begins with a capital letter and has punctuation at the end. She has children come up to the book and point to capital letters and punctuation. She tells them they will read the book again the next day, and the children go to their cubbies to get out their writing folders.

The Beginnings

Young parents are often encouraged to read to their babies as soon as they are born. Some even believe that reading to babies before they are born is helpful to a child's literacy development. The fact is, emergent literacy begins as soon as a baby is exposed to speech. Young children learn language by listening to the world around them—parents, siblings, family members, music that is played in the home, and the television.

As babies listen and learn, they begin to babble and make approximations at speech. Parents, caregivers, and siblings respond to the speech in conversational tones, using eye contact. As babbles turn into one- and two-word utterances, others in the home begin to respond to the meaning of the speech, often recasting or rephrasing. After much trial and error, young children begin to speak in complete or nearly complete sentences, and their language takes on more and more characteristics of conventional speech. I can remember Marsh saying, "Marsh pay dat" at about 18 months, when he wanted to play with a certain toy; and I can remember Missy saying, "I not go nastics" at about the same age when she wanted to leave gymnastic because she decided she didn't like her teacher's loud voice.

Children learn to read and write in much the same way—by making approximations. One of the earliest reading behaviors children display is attending to a book that is read by a parent or caregiver. They may look at the pictures and point as they listen to the story, and they slowly begin to learn many concepts about print. They see their parent turn the pages, they realize the pictures go with the story, and they eventually start to realize that the print in the book is actually talk written down.

It is very typical for young children to want to hear a favorite story over and over again. Eventually, a child may memorize part or all of the text. Marsh listened to *Go Away, Big Green Scary Monster* (Emberley, 1992) so many times when he was 2 years old, that he began to say it from memory. When Missy was born, he took pride in reading the book to her and showing her the pictures. As with many children, memorization was a gateway to reading for Marsh. As he read the book to his sister, he turned the pages starting at the front of the book and going to the back, and he pointed at the pictures for her to see. He understood that pictures help tell the story and that you always start at the front of the book and turn pages to get to the back as you read.

Similarly, children often engage in pretend reading, turning the pages of a book and telling what they expect to happen in the story, based upon the pictures. This is a very sophisticated process, and young children often tell their story in the pattern they have heard in other stories, frequently even using story language, such as "once upon a time." One child I was babysitting as a teenager pretend read *Jemima Puddle-Duck* (Potter, 1908) to me, using the words, "For the duck was very poor." This is story language that she had heard in one of her books.

At some point, usually Kindergarten or first grade, children begin to realize that print carries a message, it goes from left to right, and that for every word that is on a page, a word is read. It is helpful to provide young children with books with few words on each page and pictures that support the meaning. Little by little, as they begin to attend to the text, children recognize some words and begin to put together letters and sounds. In addition, they attend to pictures to help them get meaning from the text. They realize that book reading sounds like talk and follows the structure of speaking.

Cueing Systems

Readers use cues from the text to read and make meaning of the text. The three main cueing systems are the graphophonic, the semantic, and the syntactic cueing systems. When children use the graphophonic cueing system, they are paying attention to the sounds as they are represented with letters. Letter and sound cues are also referred to as "visual" cues (Clay, 1993). The semantic cueing system deals with the meaning of the text, and semantic cues are often called "meaning" cues. Syntactic cues, also known as "structural" cues, are the cues that relate to the structure of the text and the order of the words. Readers use the cueing systems naturally as they read. However, some children need instruction in how to recognize and use the cues. Guided Reading is helpful for students who need this type of instruction, and we will discuss it later in this chapter.

Another important type of cues is pragmatic cues. Pragmatic cues have to do with using language in different ways depending upon the setting or situation. Children learn that different language forms and levels of language formality are used in different situations (Templeton & Gehsmann, 2014). For instance, they may speak one way with their peers on the playground and another way when speaking in front of the class or to the principal.

Scaffolding

Teachers scaffold instruction to meet the needs of students and provide support they need as they learn literacy, as we discussed in Chapter 1. Similar to physical scaffolding used with building, teachers provide scaffolding for students and

slowly taper off and remove support as students become more independent. Pearson and Gallagher (1983) described gradual release of responsibility as going from maximum support to lesser support to guide students to independence. The authors coined the popular terms "I do, we do, you do." The teacher first models the task, then the whole group or small group performs the task with support from the teacher. Finally, students work on the task individually and practice as they become more and more independent.

Read-Aloud

One of the most important introductions to reading for young children is read-aloud. In fact, Shannon (2002) makes this claim, "The first rule of teaching literacy is to read to your kids" (p. 6). As parents and caregivers read aloud, children begin to understand many concepts of print, the cadence of reading, and vocabulary used in the text. In terms of gradual release of responsibility, reading aloud represents full support on the part of the teacher. Children listen as teachers, parents, or caregivers read text at a level that is more complex than children can read independently. They are exposed to vocabulary, story structure, rhyme, rhythm, onomatopoeia, various genres, and increasingly complex ideas as teachers read aloud. In addition, teachers model fluent reading and reading strategies as they read aloud and talk through the text. Layne (2015) names further benefits of reading aloud as fluency, syntactic development, comprehension, pronunciation, cultural sensitivity, improved thinking and imagination, increased engagement, and better writing. The author states, ". . . the intimacy of the read-aloud experience builds rapport between a teacher and his or her students, providing a bibliotherapeutic environment that promotes a deepening emotional intelligence" (p. 9).

> It is exciting to see children enjoy a book, especially when they are just learning about what book reading is all about. I remember my second graders enjoying read-aloud time. I always sat in a rocking chair while the students sat on the carpet to listen to the story. One particular group of boys always wanted to stand beside the chair and point to pictures in the book, touch the book, make comments about the story, and ask questions, as if they wanted to actually climb into the book. One of the boys burst into the room every day, and asked, "What are we gonna read today?" Quite the opposite was Marsh's 3-year-old classroom. One day, I was observing read-aloud time, and the teacher was reading a big book. I noticed that the children got very excited and wanted to make comments and touch the pictures as the teacher read the book. The teacher told them to sit down and be quiet, and I saw their excitement fade as they retreated to their spot on the carpet. What do you think about the two different scenarios described here?

Shared Reading

Shared reading (Holdaway, 1979) involves a book that is read aloud as a whole group or a small group. All students have access to the text, which is typically in the form of a big book, a passage written on chart paper, or a book shown on the document camera. Students and teacher read the text together, and the text is usually read multiple times over several days. The teacher reads fluently, pointing to the words, and students read along. Some students may be able to read every word, while others read what they are able to read. This provides a safe environment for students to make approximations and read along at their own level. As the book is repeated, students are able to memorize parts of the text and read

more and more fluently. The teacher provides modeling and guidance in shared reading to support students as they become successful, independent readers.

Templeton and Gehsmann (2014) suggest choosing predictable text, poems, songs, and nursery rhymes for a shared reading with emergent readers, as they are enjoyable and easy to memorize. As the shared reading experience begins, it is essential that the teacher provides a book introduction to help students make connections to their background knowledge. If the book contains ideas or content with which the students are not familiar, teachers can provide concrete examples, pictures, or videos within the book introduction. Typically, the introduction includes a picture walk, and the teacher might ask students to make predictions about the story or identify words within the text. In addition, teachers can lead students in an experience, such as going outside to look at their shadows when they are reading a book about shadows.

Shared reading is a wonderful time to teach skills within the context of literature in order to provide an authentic, meaningful context for the skills. The teacher may point out capitals and punctuation, she may focus on letters, sounds, or word boundaries, or she may ask students to identify rhyming words within the text. Templeton and Gehsmann (2014) recommend using highlighter tape, Wikki Stix, or sticky notes to highlight portions of the text for students to focus on.

If careful attention to background knowledge is provided, shared reading will provide English learners with comprehensible input and allow them to practice reading in English in a low-stress environment. Students need the shared reading experience to learn how to think and talk about text under the guidance of the teacher (Gonzalez & Miller, 2020).

Guided Reading

Many people remember with dread the days when they had to read aloud in front of the class or their reading group in a method called, "round robin" reading, which typically involved students reading a page or paragraph at a time, then the teacher calling on the person in the next seat to read. These same people probably also remember the feelings of anxiety, stress, and humiliation that came when they made a mistake and the teacher corrected them or said, "Sound it out." In addition, some people may remember reading ahead to practice their part in their head or being embarrassed for the kids who had difficulty or read word by word. Although this practice is outdated and never recommended, it is still seen in many classrooms of today (Opitz & Rasinski, 2008). Students are still being made to read in front of a group with no rehearsal or support.

On the other hand, guided reading provides students with the support they need as they read softly to themselves. In Guided Reading, teachers meet with small groups of students who read at similar levels. The teacher introduces the book and activates students' background knowledge, then students read simultaneously, but not in unison. The teacher listens to students individually as they read, and gives prompts as students make miscues. After students finish reading, the teacher typically discusses strategies used by students and gives a couple of teaching points based upon her observations. Students may then engage in word work related to the text, or they may do an extension activity for the text. A guided reading lesson focuses on what happens before, during, and after reading and typically follows this format:

Before Reading The teacher selects a book that is on the students' instructional reading level. At the instructional level, the student can read the book with 90% to 94% accuracy. The book should have enough sight words that students are able to read the book successfully with support from the book introduction and from teacher prompts. The teacher also gathers a set of books so each child can have a book and prepares a book introduction, based upon students' sight word knowledge, strategy use, and background experience. According to Clay (1993), "The child should know what the story is about before he reads it" (p. 37). The teacher leads students through a picture walk of the text, discusses the plot of the book, and has students find both familiar and unfamiliar words. The goal of the book introduction is to provide the right amount of information to enable students to read the book successfully with teacher support, sight word knowledge, and strategy use. Teachers may ask students to practice a difficult passage in the text or a part of the text that is repeated throughout.

During Reading The children read aloud independently, while the teacher listens in to students one at a time and prompts to miscues or confusions. Teachers may ask: "Do you know a word that starts with those letters?" or "Do you know a word like that?" or "What could you try?" (Clay, 1993, p. 49).

After Reading The teacher points out strategy use she observed as children read, and compliments students on ways they helped themselves throughout the reading. In addition, teachers present teaching points based upon reading strategies and encourages students to use them in the future. Teachers may also involve students in word work or vocabulary strategies based upon the reading, and typically, students will be given a choice of extension activities after the reading. The teacher encourages students to revisit the books independently by placing them in baskets or in the class library. Many times, teachers ask students to read familiar books at the beginning of a guided reading lesson for fluency practice.

According to Fountas and Pinnell (1996), "teachers can show children how to read and can support children as they read" (p. 1). With the teacher's support, students are able to develop strategies that enable them to read independently and make progress toward automaticity. As teachers observe students' reading practices, they can determine their need for strategy instruction and word work. Teachers cater to specific responses, or prompts, to meet individual students' needs, while focusing on their strengths (Fountas & Pinnell, 2017). Guided reading "gives children the opportunity to develop as individual readers while participating in a socially supported activity," (Fountas & Pinnell, 1996, p. 1). Tompkins (2014) states that guided reading provides scaffolding for students in which they are actually reading and receiving support and instruction at the same time. When teachers carefully choose books at students' instructional reading level, they can help students advance through books of increasing difficulty and help them grow as independent readers (Clay, 1993).

Guided reading is helpful for native English speakers and English learners, alike. According to Fountas and Pinnell (2017), English learners "need teachers who understand their unique profile, and they need *additional* and *different* teaching" (p. 158). In addition, Peregoy and Boyle (2008) emphasize that English learners learn successfully through guided reading because of the support provided in small group settings, engaging texts at their instructional level, and scaffolding from the teacher. Fountas and Pinnell also stress the importance of insuring books are culturally relevant to the students. As teachers prepare book introductions for English learners, it is important to use concrete objects and pictures to help students understand new concepts, and help them make connections to their prior knowledge (Fountas & Pinnell, 2017; Suits, 2003).

According to Clay (1993), students use the three main cueing systems as they read: meaning cues, structural cues, and visual cues. By prompting during the reading and directly teaching reading strategies, teachers can help students access these cueing systems. The more opportunity students have to read, the more they become proficient at using cueing systems through strategy use. Guided reading is an excellent way for students to learn strategies and grow in automaticity with the guidance of their teacher to develop into independent, fluent, strategic readers (Fountas & Pinnell, 1996). To encourage a child to use meaning cues, a teacher might say, "What would make sense here?" or "What do you think it might be?" If a teacher notes that a child needs to use visual cues, she might say, "Does it look right?" or "Do you recognize any word parts?" To activate a child's use of structural cues, a teacher could say, "Does it sound right? Or "Can we say it that way?" (p. 161). As you can see, prompts can guide students to use a particular cueing system to figure out an unknown word. With the teacher's guidance, strategy instruction, and practice, students soon begin to become more proficient in their reading.

Reading Strategies

It is beneficial for students to learn how to use specific reading strategies to help them activate the cueing systems as they read. A teacher can explicitly teach strategies as a part of a guided reading lesson during the after reading section. Additionally, strategy instruction can occur in a mini-lesson in a whole group or small group setting, or in a one-on-one session with teacher and child.

Elkonin boxes (Tompkins, 2015) are used to help children learn to listen to sounds in a word and then record those sounds as letters. The teacher asks the student to articulate the word slowly, stretching out the sounds ("caaaaaat"). Next, the teacher draws a box for each sound in a word and demonstrates to the child how to push a disc into the boxes each time a sound is heard. After saying the word slowly and pushing the discs a couple of times, the teacher asks the student, "What did you hear?" "How will you write it?" and "Where will you put it?" The teacher then asks the student to write the letters in each box to write the word (c-a-t), then read the whole word. It is a good idea to have the student locate the word in a book after writing it to help make a connection between reading and writing (Clay, 1993; Hoyt, 2000; McGee & Richgels, 2008; Reutzel & Cooter, 2003; Tompkins, 2014). Eventually, the teacher can ask children to listen to the sounds they hear in a word, hold up a finger for each sound, then draw their own boxes to push the discs into as they figure out a word.

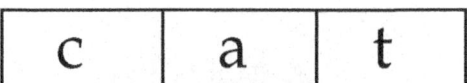

Making and breaking words comes from Reading Recovery (Clay, 1993) and helps a child to see how words work, and how you can read or write a new word by changing up a known word. The teacher gives the child the magnetic letters to make a word they know, then asks them to make the word and read it. Next, the teacher demonstrates for the child how they can make another word by changing one letter in the word. For instance, she might start with the word "look," then change the "l" to a "b" to make the word "book." The child then reads the new word, and the teacher again changes the first letter to make "cook," "took," and "hook." Each time, the child reads the new word. After the teacher shows the child the process, she then asks the child to move the letters to make each new word and read them. Again, it is beneficial to have children locate the words in a book to make the connection to literature.

Analogies take making and breaking words to the written level. Analogies can come from a child's reading or writing (Clay, 1993). This strategy helps children

read and write unknown words by making connections to words they already know. The teacher asks the child to write a known word, such as "like" and then read it. Next, the teacher says, "If you can write 'like,' you can also write 'bike.' If you can write 'bike,' you can also write 'hike,' etc." As with the other strategies, it is important to have the child find the words in a book or in their own writing.

In my pile/your pile, the teacher makes word cards using known words, then adds a few new words the child is learning (Clay, 1993). The child reads the stack of cards as quickly as possible. If the words are read correctly, they go into the child's pile, but if they are read incorrectly, they go into the teacher's pile. The teacher can then review the words in her pile, then give the child another chance to read them. New words can be added to the stack as the child's repertoire of words increases. My pile/your pile helps children learn to read sight words automatically, which may be more difficult for English learners as many sight words are either exceptions to known spelling rules, or they may be abstract (Tompkins, 2014). Starting with known words and adding a few new words at a time enables children to experience success with this strategy.

Children can learn to look for "chunks," or combinations of letters often found together, in unknown words they are trying to read (Clay, 1993). For example, children can read "landing" if they know "an," "and," "land," and "ing." Teachers can prompt children to use the chunking strategy by saying, "Find a part you know," "Can you find a little word in that big word?" or "Chunk the word." Children can also underline chunks found in words they are trying to read or sort words by placing words with a certain chunk into a pile (Bear, Invernizzi, Templeton, & Johnston, 2008).

Children can make strategy tents by folding a large index card or piece of tag board in half to make a "tent" that can be placed on their desk or table while they are reading. The teacher can help children brainstorm different things they can do to help themselves as they are reading. Next, children write some strategies on their tents. It is helpful if they draw a small picture to go with each strategy to help them recall the information. As children are reading, they can refer to their strategy tents so they can remember the strategies that help them read. A variation is to make strategy bookmarks. Hoyt (2000) calls these 'Fix-It' bookmarks. Children may include strategies such as "reread," "check the picture," or "think about the story."

Independent Reading

Independent reading is the important block of time during which children orchestrate sight words, strategies, cueing systems, and everything else they know about reading, as they read quietly or silently by themselves. Independent reading occurs with little support from the teacher, and it is a time for students to practice reading books they enjoy. Just as basketball, dance, singing, or playing an instrument require practice, reading must be practiced as well, in order to become proficient (Allington, 1977; Anderson, Wilson, & Fielding, 1988; Krashen, 2004; Templeton & Gehsmann, 2014). It is essential for children to have uninterrupted, sustained time every day for independent reading.

Teachers often provide special areas with carpet and pillows where children can relax while they read. One teacher I know had a reading castle in which children could read, and I used to have a reading bathtub, complete with pillows, in my classroom. It is important to have an organized way to monitor and insure all children get a turn in the special reading areas. It is also enjoyable to take children outside to read on a nice day or have children bring sleeping bags and pillows to school for a special day when they get to read for larger than usual amounts of time.

For emergent readers, independent reading is not a quiet time, but there is a busy hum in the room, as silent reading is a skill that comes later. Templeton and Gehsmann (2014) suggest talking to very young children about what independent reading time can look like. The authors encourage children to look at pictures and think about the story, read familiar books, read from memory, or read the room.

"Reading the room" refers to children reading any environmental print in the room, the word wall, the calendar, the alphabet chart, or any other print that might be found on the walls or in the room. Children can even read quietly with a partner at this time.

A child's independent reading level is a text level at which they can read with 95% or better accuracy without support from the teacher (Fountas & Pinnell, 1996). When children are able to accurately read 95% of a text, their comprehension improves (Sinatra, Brown, & Reynolds, 2002). Ideally, all children will be reading a book at their independent level during independent reading time. Teachers can help children find books at the independent level by carefully monitoring their books levels, words they know, and strategies they use and guiding them through the book selection process. It is important that children are allowed to choose their own books for independent reading time. Teachers can help by offering a well-stocked, inviting classroom library that includes books that cater to a wide variety of interests and levels. Multicultural books and books that represent the ethnicities of all students in the class should be included. Additionally, it is a good idea to provide both fiction and nonfiction books, comic books, manga, and graphic novels, so all children will find something to read that they enjoy.

English learners, in particular, benefit from reading books with rich vocabulary. The bulk of vocabulary learning occurs when a child has access to high-quality reading material and reads for a sustained time every day, rather than from direct vocabulary instruction (Cunningham & Zibulsky, 2014). In addition, English learners' language acquisition is improved through having many opportunities for independent reading practice (Krashen, 1993). Miller and Moss (2013) state "Independent reading is an essential practice, one that develops background knowledge, improves fluency and comprehension, heightens motivation, increases reading achievement, and helps students broaden their vocabulary" (pp. 11, 12). Independent reading time is also the time during which children become enthusiastic, passionate readers. Gallagher (2009) stresses, "When schools deprive students of the pleasures of recreational reading, we end up graduating test-takers who may never again read for pleasure" (p. 45). Independent reading is important for hooking children on reading and for helping them to become lifelong readers.

Emergent readers need a classroom environment that immerses them in print, reading, and writing. It is important for teachers to scaffold students as they learn to read in order to provide the support needed as they grow as readers. In this chapter we have talked about scaffolding reading from read-aloud to shared reading, then to guided reading, and finally, independent reading. In the next chapter we will discuss how students learn to write, and how teachers can scaffold them as they become writers.

References

Allington, R. (1977). If they don't get to read much, how they ever gonna get good? *Journal of Reading, 21,* 57–61.

Anderson, R., Wilson, P., & Fielding, L. (1988). Growth in reading and how children spend their time outside of school. *Reading Research Quarterly, 23,* 285–303.

Bear, D., Invernizzi, M., Templeton, S., & Johnston, F. (2008). *Words their way: Word study for phonics, vocabulary, and spelling instruction.* Upper Saddle River, NJ: Pearson/Merrill/Prentice Hall.

Clay, M. (1993). *Reading Recovery: A guidebook.* Portsmouth, NH: Heinemann.

Cunningham, A., & Zibulsky, J. (2014). *Book smart: How to develop and support successful, motivated readers.* New York: Oxford University Press.

Emberley, E. (1992). *Go away big green monster.* Boston, MA: Little, Brown and Company.

Fountas, I., & Pinnell, G. (1996). Guided reading: *Good first teaching for all children.* Portsmouth, NH: Heinemann.

Fountas, I., & Pinnell, G. (2001). *Guided readers and writers: Teaching comprehension, genre, and content literacy.* Portsmouth, NH: Heinemann.

Fountas, I., & Pinnell, G. (2017). *Guided reading: Responsive teaching across the grades.* Portsmouth, NH: Heinemann.

Gallagher, K. (2009). *Readicide: How schools are killing reading and what you can do about it.* Portland, ME: Stenhouse Publishers.

Gonzalez, V., & Miller, M. (2020). *Reading and writing with English learners.* San Clemente, CA: Seidlitz Education.

Holdaway, D. (1979). *The foundations of literacy.* Sydney: Ashton Scholastic.

Hoyt, L. (2000). *Snapshots: Literacy mini-lessons up close.* Portsmouth, NH: Heinemann.

Krashen, S. (1993). The case for free voluntary reading. *Canadian Modern Language Review, 50*, 72–82.

Krashen, S. (2004). *The power of reading: Insights from the research.* (2nd ed). Portsmoth, NH: Heinemann.

Layne, S. (2015). *In defense of read-aloud: Sustaining best practice.* Portland, ME: Stenhouse Publishers.

McGee, L., & Richgels, D. (2008). *Literacy's beginnings: Supporting young readers and writers.* Boston, MA: Allyn & Bacon/Pearson.

Miller, D., & Moss, B. (2013). *No more independent reading without support.* Portsmouth, NH: Heinemann.

Noble, T. (1980). *The day Jimmy's boa ate the wash.* New York: Penguin.

Optiz, M. & Rasiniski, T. (2008). *Good-bye round robin: 25 effective oral reading strategies.* Portsmouth, NH: Heinemann.

Pearson, P. D., & Gallagher, M. (1983). The instruction of reading comprehension. *Contemporary Educational Psychology, 8*, 317--344.

Peregoy, S., & Boyle, O. (2008). *Reading, writing, and learning in ESL: A resource book for K-12 teachers* (5th ed.). Boston, MA: Allyn & Bacon/Pearson.

Potter, B. (1908). *The tale of Jemima Puddle-Duck.* New York: Frederick Warne & Co.

Reutzel, R., & Cooter, R. (2003). *Strategies for reading assessment and instruction: Helping every child succeed.* Upper Saddle River, NJ: Merrill/Prentice Hall.

Sendak, M. (1964). *Where the wild things are.* New York: Harper & Row.

Shannon, P. (2002). The myths of reading aloud. *The Dragon Lode, 202*, 6–11.

Sinatra, G., Brown, K., & Reynolds, R. (2002). Implications of cognitive resources for comprehension strategies instruction. In C.C. Block & M. Pressley (Eds.), *Comprehension instruction: Research-based practices* (pp. 62–76). New York: Guilford.

Suits, B. (2003). Guided reading and second-language learners. *Multicultural Education, 11*(2), 27–34.

Templeton, S., & Gehsmann, K. (2014). *Teaching reading and writing: The developmental approach.* Boston, MA: Pearson.

Tompkins, G. (2014). *Literacy for the 21st Century: A balanced approach.* Boston, MA: Pearson.

Tompkins, G. (2015). *Literacy in the early grades: A successful start for Pre-K-4 readers and writers.* Boston: Pearson.

CHAPTER 3

Learning to Write

Mr. Martinez calls his Kindergartners to the carpet at the front of the class. He has previously talked to them about making a list of things they love, and today, he has asked them to bring their list to the carpet with them. The children eagerly find a spot on the carpet, clutching their lists and wait to hear what their teacher has to say. He starts by telling them he wants them to choose a topic from their list to write about, and he will show them how. He shows his list on the document camera, and reads the topics one by one. He vocalizes the thoughts he has as he goes down the list, "I could write about my dog. I could tell a great story about my dog. Or maybe I will write about fishing at the pond. That was really fun. But I think I will write about my cat and her new toy. I could really tell a funny story about that!" Mr. Martinez circles "My cat and her new toy" in red marker. Next, he asks the students to talk to their shoulder partners about which of their topics they want to choose to write about. Afterward, he asks students to go back to their tables and choose a red crayon. He says, "Now, I want you to choose the topic you will write about today and draw a circle around it with your red crayon." Students excitedly choose their red crayons and circle their topic of choice. "Now," says Mr. Martinez, "I would like all of you to take your writing notebook and write about the topic you circled." Students begin to draw pictures and write letters in their notebooks. Some of them write a few words, and others draw pictures and label them with a couple of letters. They work for several minutes, chatting with table mates as they work. After about 10 minutes, Mr. Martinez notices that most students seem to be finished with their writing pieces, so he asks them to share their writing with their shoulder partners. Students happily tell their partners about what they have written.

The Beginnings

When a child begins to make scribbles and drawings, they are in the earliest stages of writing. Young children often tell stories and draw or scribble as they talk. They are understanding that writing is talk written down. For example, I once had a student named David who loved to tell me stories about a cat chasing a mouse. He drew the mouse with the cat close on its tail on his dry erase board. Then he erased the mouse because it ran into the hole, and he erased the cat because it went away when the mouse went into the hole. At the end of the story, there was nothing there because both the mouse and the cat went away, but it was David's story, and he was excited about it. After representing their writing with drawings, children may soon begin to label drawings with letters that represent words. Eventually, the young child will begin to represent words with one or two letters. These are all the beginnings of writing. Children understand that print carries a message, and when they are making marks on the page, it has meaning to them.

> I have heard parents say things like, "That is not writing. That's just scribbles" to their young child (3 or 4 years old), and then try to teach the child to write conventional letters. How would you explain to a parent that their child is going through the expected stages of reading and writing? What would you tell them to do in order to support their child in learning to write?

Teachers of young children can provide a variety of writing utensils and different kinds and colors of paper for children to draw and write on. They should be encouraged to have conversations with their peers as they experiment with writing. In addition, writing supplies should be available in the home center, so students can use writing in purposeful ways, such as making shopping lists or menus. Marsh and Missy and their six cousins used to make menus, then come and "take our order" when the adults were sitting around. They were all different ages and were at all levels of writing, but even the youngest wrote down our orders in a very businesslike way. They disappeared to the toy kitchen, then came back with play food for us on a book they were using for a tray. They understood that people in restaurants read menus, and that waiters take people's orders by writing something down. They also understood that print carries a message, and that they can represent meaning by writing something down.

Marsh and Missy also made libraries in their closets. They made library cards to go in each of their books, and put a piece of paper in the back of the book for a date stamp. My husband and I came to check out books, and we were to write down our names on the cards. They took our cards, then stamped the due date in the back of the book. They paid attention to the process of checking out a book from the library and how writing was used as part of that process. Children naturally imitate reading and writing events they see happening around them, and this helps them develop as emergent readers and writers. Teachers can take advantage of students' natural curiosity with print by providing many materials and opportunities for them to experiment with print in the classroom.

Cooper and Kiger (2003) recommend that teachers of emergent writers teach through the modes of writing, which are based on Pearson's (1985) notion of Gradual Release of Responsibility from teacher to student. The modes of writing include write-aloud, shared writing, and independent writing. Teachers model metacognition, skills, and procedures; then they guide the children through the writing process through shared writing. Ultimately, the children write independently, putting together all they have learned about writing. It is essential to provide a sustained time for students to practice writing every day, just as they have a daily sustained time for independent reading.

Write-Aloud

In a write-aloud, the teacher verbalizes her thoughts as a writer while modeling the writing process. She talks through what is going on in her head as she writes. Graves (1983) states, "The objective of composing before children is to make explicit what children ordinarily can't see: how words go down on paper, and the thoughts that go with the decisions made in writing" (p. 45). The teacher can write aloud using a document camera, chart paper, or the whiteboard while students are seated on the floor.

While writing aloud, the teacher does most of the talking, so it is a good idea for children to have many chances to turn and talk to their shoulder partners about what the teacher is saying and doing. As the teacher is writing, it is helpful for her to stop frequently to have children chorally read portions of the text. Chorally reading and talking to peers will also provide support for English learners. It is also good for the teacher to write using high-frequency words that the children can read. This also enables English learners to make connections to what they already know. Write-aloud is a powerful tool that allows children to witness how ideas grow into a piece of writing.

Routman (1994) recommends doing a "Morning Message" as a write-aloud. The teacher models writing the happenings of the day while asking such questions as, "Why did I capitalize . . .? Why did I begin the paragraph here? Why did I use a comma? and What did you notice about . . .?" (p. 51). Students and teacher discuss the writing as the teacher writes aloud. One second grade teacher told Routman, "I feel writing aloud with my students clearly puts so many of the conventions we want to teach children in the proper context of written language without teaching the skills in isolation" (p. 52).

When students see their teachers write, they are less intimidated by writing, and they are more motivated to write (Fletcher & Portalupi, 2001). Students become better writers the more they see their teacher write (Routman, 1994), and they begin to understand what is expected of them as writers. As Cooper (2000) suggests, teachers can teach the writing process through write-aloud. In fact, write-aloud can be used for students at any grade level to teach new types of writing, and to teach writer's craft. Graves (1983) describes how he and his students became a community of writers when he wrote aloud with them. He and his students supported and encouraged each other through the problem solving involved in the writing process.

Shared Writing

In shared writing, teacher and students compose a text together. Tompkins and Collom (2004) explain that shared writing is "the bridge between more teacher-directed (modeled) writing and independent writing" (p. iii). One type of shared writing is the Language Experience Approach in which the students participate in a shared experience, such as baking a cake or going on a field trip, and dictate a story to the teacher (Ashton-Warner, 1963) about their experiences. The teacher writes down the students' words on chart paper, a document camera, or a whiteboard; and stops to ask questions about what a word begins with or whether or not it should be capitalized. Students then read the writing piece chorally, and the teacher typically places the finished story in the book center for students to read on their own or in pairs.

Interactive Writing is the second type of shared writing. In interactive writing, students and teacher both do the writing (McKenzie, 1985). Students write the words they know, and the teacher writes unknown words. Teachers sometimes use correction tape to correct words that are misspelled so the writing piece will serve as an example of correct writing. Other teachers choose to leave the writing as it is. The teacher can lead students in the spelling of words by asking questions such as, "How many sounds are in that word?" and "What letters to we use to write down those sounds?" It is a good idea to let all students write the words or sentences on individual dry erase boards or paper to practice what is being written by the class (Tompkins & Collom, 2004), as well as to make sure all students stay engaged.

Shared writing is "an excellent technique for young ELLs who are at the beginning stage of writing and learning the alphabet, letter formation, and letter-sound correspondence" (Wright, 2015, p. 239). Shared writing allows teachers to cater the lesson to English learners' needs (Tompkins & Collom, 2004) and introduce skills for individual learners, such as concepts about print, vocabulary, punctuation, spelling, and phonics (Gonzales & Miller, 2020). English learners are able to see a demonstration of the composing process during interactive writing, just as they are with write-aloud. As in write-aloud, there is heavy teacher support, but students are able to practice writing letters and words and reading what has been written along with their peers in a nonthreatening environment.

Tompkins (2015) explains that shared writing provides writing experiences for students who are not yet able to write independently. According to Routman (2000), "Shared writing builds on what the teacher has already been modeling through write-aloud" (p. 37). The Language Experience Approach and Interactive Writing allow students the opportunity to participate in writing before they are expected to write independently, and both approaches come from the idea that students are able to read pieces of literature that they were involved in composing (Tompkins & Collom, 2004). As in write-aloud, students are able to see and hear the thought processes involved in writing during shared writing.

Further, Routman (2005) states that shared writing enables a teacher to serve as "expert and scribe for her apprentices" as they learn to enjoy the composing process and become more confident in expressing themselves (p. 83). As students dictate ideas, the teacher can expand on those ideas and demonstrate complete sentences and organized writing.

Independent Writing

In independent writing, we move from heavy teacher support to less teacher support. The most important elements of teaching children to write are time, choice, and response or feedback (Atwell, 1987; Routman, 1994; Wood & Dickinson, 2000). Students should be able to choose the topic and genre (Bright, 1995) of their writing. They should be allowed to write about things they know and things that interest them so they will feel ownership over their writing (Tompkins, 2015). In addition, students need sustained time at school to write every day. They should be working with their peers and their teacher, who collaborate, confer, and respond to their writing (Calkins, 1983; Cambourne, 1995). Writing workshop (Atwell,

1987; Graves, 1983) incorporates all of these elements, and Cooper and Kiger (2003) described writing workshop as "a flexible plan that places students and teacher in a partnership for learning" (p. 442).

Possible components of writing workshop are mini-lessons, status-of-the-class reports, writing and conferring time, and group sharing (Atwell, 1987). Mini-lessons are short, concise lessons that focus on one specific skill, strategy, or procedure and typically last 10 to 15 minutes. Many teachers use status-of-the-class reports to quickly check what each student is working on in writing workshop. This insures each child knows what they are supposed to be working on and holds them accountable. Writing and conferring time is when students write at various stages of the writing process and engage in conferences with peers and teacher. Group sharing occurs at the end of writing workshop, and several students are invited to share their writing and receive feedback from the whole group. (Higgins, Miller, & Wegmann, 2007).

According to Tompkins (1994), "The writing process is a way of looking at writing instruction in which the emphasis is shifted from students' finished products to what students think and do as they write" (p. 7). Murray (1972) described writing as a process and stressed that the focus should be on the process of writing rather than the finished product. Tompkins (2015) further states that writing workshop "is the best way to implant the writing process" (p. 359). In writing workshop, students participate in the writing process by selecting their own topics, then engage in prewriting activities, such as graphic organizers or brainstorming. Next, they begin drafting, then confer with peers and teacher. During these conferences, students give and get suggestions for revision and editing, so they can perfect their writing piece into a final copy or published book. Flower and Hayes (1981) and Hayes and Flower (1986) identified three components of the writing process as planning, translating, and reviewing. Atwell (1987) and Cooper and Kiger (2003) identified five components: prewriting and planning, drafting, revising, editing, and publishing. During prewriting and planning, students choose topics, brainstorm ideas, and develop a writing plan. While drafting, students write without interruption and are encouraged to get their thoughts down on paper and worry about spelling and correctness later. While revising, students make changes in the writing, adding more details and elaborating on ideas. During the editing process, students correct their writing piece for spelling, punctuation, and other writing conventions. In the publishing stage, students publish their writing in some way, such as making a book or writing a final draft of a letter.

In an elementary school where I used to teach, students chose one of their published writing pieces to share at the Young Authors' Day Celebration. Parents, siblings, grandparents, and administrators came to hear children read their writing pieces. Each child sat at a table, and visitors milled around the room stopping to listen to children read their pieces. Each child read their piece two or three times to different audiences. Afterward, everyone enjoyed refreshments. This celebration was a fun culmination of all of the writing students did during the year. It can even be done more than once a year. The students looked forward to this day and were so excited to share their masterpieces!

All students, including very young children and English learners, can learn to think and write using the writing process (Tompkins, 2015). During Writing Workshop time, the classroom becomes a community of writers guided by the teacher (Tompkins, 2015). The writing process is, by nature, differentiated. Students work at their own level and write about what interests them, while teachers cater to individual needs through conferences and mini-lessons. Writers need a sustained time every day to orchestrate their thinking and all they know about the composing process.

References

Ashton-Warner, S. (1963). *Teacher.* New York: Simon & Schuster.

Atwell, N. (1987). *In the middle: Writing, reading, and learning with adolescents.* Portsmouth, NH: Boynton/Cook.

Atwell, N. (1998). *In the middle: New understandings about writing, reading, and learning* (2nd ed). Portsmouth, NH: Heinemann.

Bright, R. (1995). *Writing instruction in the intermediate grades: What is said, what is done, what is understood.* Newark, DE: International Reading Association.

Calkins, L. M. (1983). *Lessons from a child: On the teaching and learning of writing.* Portsmouth, NH: Heinemann.

Cambourne, B. (1995). Toward an educationally relevant theory of literacy learning: Twenty years of inquiry. *The Reading Teacher, 49,* 182–190.

Cooper, J. D. (2000). *Literacy: Helping children construct meaning.* Boston: Houghton Mifflin.

Cooper, J. (2003). *Literacy assessment: Helping children construct meaning.* Boston, MA: Houghton Mifflin Harcourt.

Cooper, J., & Kiger, N. (2003). *Literacy: Helping children construct literacy.* Boston, MA: Houghton Mifflin.

Fletcher, R., & Portalupi, J. (2001). *Writing workshop: The essential guide.* Portsmouth, NH: Heinemann.

Flower, L., & Hayes, J. (1981). A cognitive process theory of writing. *College Composition and Communication, 32,* 365–387.

Gonzales, V., & Miller, M. (2020). *Reading and writing with English learners: A framework for K-5.*

Graves, D. (1983). *Writing: Teachers and children at work.* Portsmouth, NH: Heinemann.

Hayes, J., & Flower, L. (1986). Writing research and the writer. *American Psychologist, 41,* 1106–1113.

Higgins, B., Miller, M., & Wegmann (2006). Teaching to the test...not: Balancing best practice and testing requirements in writing. *The Reading Teacher, 60* (4).

McKenzie, M. (1985). Shared writing: Apprenticeship in writing. *Language Matters, 1* (2), 1–5.

Murray, D. (1972). Teach Writing as a Process Not Product. *The Leaflet* (November 1972),rpt. in *Cross-Talk in Comp Theory,* 2nd ed., ed. Victor Villanueva, Urbana: NCTE, 2003.

Pearson, P. D. (1985). Changing the face of reading comprehension. *The Reading Teacher, 38,* 724–738.

Routman, R. (1994). *Invitations: Changing as teachers and learners K-12.* Portsmouth, NH: Heinemann.

Routman, R. (2000). *Conversations: Strategies for teaching, learning, and evaluating.* Portsmouth, NJ: Heinemann.

Routman, R. (2005). *Writing essentials: Raising expectations and results while simplifying teaching.* Portsmouth, NH: Heinemann.

Tompkins, G. (1994). *Teaching writing: Balancing process and product.* New York: Macmillan. University.

Tompkins, G. (2015). *Literacy in the early grades: A successful start for preK-4 readers and writers.* Boston, MA: Pearson.

Tompkins, G., & Collom, S. (2004). *Sharing the pen: Interactive writing with young children.* Upper Saddle River, NJ: Pearson Merrill Prentice Hall.

Wood, K., & Dickinson, T. (2000). *Promoting literacy in grades 4-9: A handbook for teachers and administrators.* Boston, MA: Allyn & Bacon.

Wright, W. (2015). *Foundations for teaching English language learners: Research, theory, policy, and practice.* Philadelphia, PA: Caslon Publishing.

CHAPTER 4

Reading and Writing in the Classroom

Ms. Johnson reads the big book Sheep in a Jeep *(Shaw, 1986) to her first grade class to begin her mini-lesson on rhyming words at the start of Reading Workshop. They talk about the various rhyming words in the book, then Ms. Johnson writes them on the dry erase board. Next, she tells the students she will say a word, then toss a beanbag to someone. That person is to say a word that rhymes with the original word, then toss it to someone else, who says another rhyming word. She says, "cat" and tosses the beanbag to Jaime. Jaime says, "bat" and tosses the ball to Meagan. Meagan says, "rat" and tosses the ball to Logan. Logan says, "sat" and tosses the ball to Alma, and so on. Ms. Johnson then gives each group a set of magnetic letters and asks them to make "cat." After she sees that each group has made "cat," she asks them to take away the "c" and replace it with "b." As students remove the "c" and put a "b," they start to say, "bat." Ms. Johnson then says, "Turn to your shoulder partner and read that word." All students turn to their shoulder partners and read, "bat." She then asks them to make "rat," and "sat" and follows the same sequence. Next, Ms. Johnson asks students to take out their individual dry erase boards. She asks them to write "cat" and checks to see that everyone has written "cat." Then she has them read the word aloud. Next, she says, "If you can write 'cat,' you can write 'bat.'" All students write "bat." Then she asks them to all read the word "bat." Then she says, "If you can write 'bat,' you can write 'rat'" and so on. Next, Ms. Johnson writes "cat," "bat," "sat," and "rat" on sentence strips and places them on the word wall. Then as she points to the words, the class reads them together. She then tells the students, "It is now time to start DEAR. Please look and see if you see any of the rhyming words we talked about today while you were reading. Remember, if you know a word, you can read and write a word that rhymes with that word."* All students take their books and find a spot to read silently or quietly.

In a balanced literacy classroom, students are given sustained times to practice orchestrating all they know about reading and writing during reading and writing workshops. In addition, they have time with their teacher to learn the strategies and skills involved in reading and writing. Teachers scaffold students' understanding of what good readers and writers do through mini-lessons, modeling, write-alouds, shared writing, read-aloud, shared reading, guided reading, and word work. Students also participate in literacy centers to practice all that is involved in reading and writing.

Phonics

Before children are able to use phonics, they must first develop phonological awareness, which is the understanding that speech is made up of sounds. Under the umbrella of phonological awareness is phonemic awareness, which is "the ability to divide syllables into the smallest units of sound" (Bear, Invernizzi, Templeton, & Johnston, 2004). Phonics is "the set of relationships between phonology, the sounds in speech, and orthography, the spelling system" (Tompkins, 2015, p. 115), and it is an important part of both reading and writing. Phonemes are the smallest unit of speech sound and are represented as letters or letter combinations, called graphemes. For example, the phoneme /s/ is represented with the grapheme "s," and the phoneme /sh/ is represented with the grapheme "sh." When a child associates sounds with letters, and they are able to record sounds as letters to create words, they are using phonics. When a child recognizes letters and the sounds they make, then reads across a word from left to right putting the sounds together, they are also using phonics to "sound out" the word, and they are applying the alphabetic principle. However, readers cannot rely on graphophonic cues alone, as they must use the other cueing systems as well, because many words cannot be sounded out ("through," "light," etc.). Students must also use the semantic (meaning) and syntactic (structure) cueing systems along with the graphophonic cueing system, which focuses on phonics. "In other words, phonics instruction is essential for students to learn to read and write, but it is not sufficient on its own" (Gonzalez & Miller, 2020, p.).

Armbruster, Lehr, and Osborn (2001) state that phonemic awareness provides the foundation for phonics and spelling. Strategies for developing phonemic awareness include identifying sounds, categorizing sounds, substituting sounds, blending, and segmenting. One thing a teacher can do to help students learn to identify sounds in words is to throw a ball to a student and say "What sound do you hear at the beginning of 'sat'?" The student answers and tosses the ball back.

To categorize sounds, students can place objects into different piles depending upon the letter they begin with. Teachers can also read poems and rhyming books to children to expose them to rhyming words, then talk about words that rhyme within the book or poem. After students have become accustomed to listening and identifying rhymes, the teacher can say a word and toss the ball to several students who, in turn, will say words that rhyme with the teacher's word, as in the scenario.

To work on substituting sounds, the teacher can say, "Say 'cat.' Now take away the /c/ and replace it with /s/" to encourage students to say the new "sat." Teaching students the concept of onset and rime helps to them to think about substituting sounds, how words work, and how to recognize word families. The onset is the consonant at the beginning of a one-syllable word (if any), and the rime is made up of all the letters that follow the consonant. For example, in the word *cat*, /c/ is the onset, and /at/ is the rime. Onset and rime can be done orally to help develop phonemic awareness, or in writing, using phonics. Making and Breaking words and Analogies are two activities that can be used to teach word families when the child is ready to use phonics, and they are discussed in this chapter.

To help children learn to blend sounds to make a word, the teacher can have the children guess a riddle. For example, the teacher could say, "I am an animal with fur. I say 'meow' and my name sounds like /c/ /a/ /t/. What am I?" The students can use the clues and blend the sounds to make the word "cat." After several rounds of riddles, students can make their own riddles to share with each other. This can eventually be done as a bridge to phonics, using magnetic letters to spell each word after the riddle is guessed.

Teachers can help students learn to segment words into beginning, middle, and ending sounds by having them say a word, then hold up one finger for every sound they hear, then say the sounds. Students can also do a ball toss to have one child say the first sound of a word, one say the middle sound, and one say the ending sound.

Bear et al. (2004) recommend using word sorts to develop both phonemic awareness and phonics. For phonemic awareness, children can sort pictures by the letter they begin with. "Picture sorts offer more than traditional worksheets," (p. 63), according to the authors, as they are hands-on, they can be differentiated for different children, and they can be used over and over. In addition, a typical worksheet might have six or seven pictures to match, while a picture sort might have three times as many pictures to sort.

Word sorts can be used for phonics applications, patterns, meaning, and concepts (Bear et al., 2004). Children can sort according to chunks or word families with cards containing the words, or they can sort by meaning using words that are homophones or homographs, or by roots, stems, and affixes. For concept sorts, students can sort by words that belong together, such as animal words, transportation words, or food words. In addition, words can be written by the students in a sort.

Teachers can support a child's phonemic awareness by using songs, poetry books, wordplay books, alphabet books, word games, rhyming books, and rhyming games. Pinnell and Fountas (1998) suggest using letter books made by the teacher. The letter is written on the front of the book and each page has a picture of something that begins with that letter. A child can read through the book by saying the names of each picture, and it helps them to associate the letter with the sound. Pinnell and Fountas state, "The child is saying and hearing a series of words that begin with the same sound, thereby developing phonemic awareness" (p. 141).

Commercially made alphabet books can be very useful for students learning to apply phonics. Pinnell and Fountas (1998) suggest placing several in the book center and giving children access to magnetic letters so they can begin to make connections between the sounds and letters. Students can also have access to pencils and markers, so they can write the letters they are seeing in the alphabet books. In addition, teachers can help students make their own alphabet books, starting with the letters and sounds they know. The teacher can help the child write the letters they know, then pick out stickers or pictures of something that begins with that letter or draw their own pictures. Index cards with a hole punched can be fastened with a ring, and letters be added as they are learned. The child can read through the alphabet book to practice saying the letters and words until they have mastered the whole alphabet.

Children's names can also be useful in learning the sounds of letters. Children's names are very personal and important to them (Pinnell & Fountas, 1998). In fact, one child named John in my preschool class became upset when he realized Jessica also had a "J" in her name. He exclaimed, "That's mine!" It is also very easy for children to learn letter patterns that appear in their own names. Marsh had an easy time learning both the "ar" chunk and the "sh" chunk because they are in his name. It is helpful to have a name chart in the room and to label cubbies and workspaces with names. Children immediately recognize their own names, and they quickly learn to recognize each other's names in writing.

As children are learning letters and sounds, teachers can give them many different opportunities to experiment with making the letters and sounds together. The teacher can set up a series of centers for students to experience letters with different mediums. One center could contain glue and glitter to make different letters on a piece of construction paper. Another center could have shaving cream to write different letters, and another could have a dry erase board with markers. Children should be encouraged to make the sound of each letter as they create them. When students are lining up to go home or on the way to the cafeteria, the class can practice air writing letters and making the sounds, or they can look for letters on the walls of the school and name them and make the sounds.

It is important to show children phonics examples in the context of literature and through writing instruction. For instance, when a child learns a sound or word, the teacher can show that sound or word in a book the class is reading. As the class is creating a language experience story, the teacher can say, for example, "What sound does 'went' start with? What letter do we use to make that sound?"

Word Work

When students are learning to apply phonics, it is essential for them to engage in various types of word work. We have already talked about word sorts, which are one form of word work. In the following paragraphs, we will see some more examples that are helpful for children to learn how words work.

Hearing and Recording Sounds in Words

For words that can be sounded out, children can use the Elkonin boxes, as we discussed in Chapter 2, to help them work on hearing and recording sounds in words. Again, this strategy is done using small plastic counters or coins (the transparent-colored disks used for counters in math work well). Start by drawing a box on the page for each sound in the word. Have the child articulate the word slowly, stretching out the sounds. Then show the child how to push the counters into the boxes each time they hear a sound. After saying the word slowly and pushing the counters a couple of times, ask the child, "What did you hear? How will you write it? Where will you put it?" This strategy will come in handy when a child needs to write an unknown word. Words in which one can hear every letter in the word (milk, cat, pig) work best for the sound boxes. Irregular words (through, thought) will not work with this strategy. It is a good idea to have the child locate the word in a book after it has been written to help them make a connection to literature.

Making and Breaking Words

We briefly discussed making and breaking words in Chapter 2, and it is also a helpful strategy to use during word work time. Making and breaking words comes from Reading Recovery (Clay, 1993). For making and breaking, give the child enough magnetic letters to make a word they know and ask them to make the word. Then ask them to read the word and run their finger under it as they read it. Next show the child that another word can be made by changing one letter in the word. Have the child make the new word, and again run their finger under it and read it slowly. Continue with other examples that can replace the changed letter. For example, if the child makes "like," it can be changed to "hike," Mike," bike," etc. Always have the child locate the known word in a book after the activity, to link the strategy back to the text. This technique can be used for adding inflections, or changing the menial vowel, as well. According to Marie Clay, one should "create a link between what the child knows and something new and go back to what the child knows in order to make a link to another known word" (Clay, 1993, p. 44). Making and breaking words helps a child to see how words work and how you can read or write a new word when you look at how a known word is put together.

Analogies

Analogies can be pulled from a child's reading or writing. They are very similar to making and breaking words, but they are written. For an analogy, take a known word and ask the child to write it. For instance, "look." Then say, "If you can write 'look,' you can also write 'book'; "If you can write 'book,' you can also write 'cook,'" and so on. Always go back and have the child read the original known word and go back to the text or the child's writing to find the word. This strategy teaches a child how to read and spell unknown words using words that they already know. Teachers can also pull words from a language experience story written by the class to show examples of word families. For instance, if the class has written the word "day" in their story, the teacher can have students write the word "day" on a practice piece of paper or an individual whiteboard, then say, "If you can write 'day,' you can also write 'way'" and so on. Word families can also be written on charts and hung on the walls for reference. Pinnell and Fountas (1998) point out, "Relying on analogies between words enables readers and writers to make leaps in learning as they use phonemic, visual, and morphemic strategies to solve words" (p. 78).

Chunks

If a child can learn "chunks," or parts of words that are often found together, they can look for those parts in unknown words that they are trying to read. For instance, a child can read "farmer," if they know "ar," "er," "arm," or "farm." You can prompt a child to use this strategy by saying, "Find a part you know," or "Can you find a little word in that big word?" You can practice this strategy by having the children do a word sort, placing all of the words that contain a certain chunk in a certain pile. You can also brainstorm words with a certain chunk and make a chart to hang up in the room. Another way you can practice the use of chunks is to write out several unknown words that have chunks in them, and let the child underline the parts they know to try figure out the word. Always remember, let the child see examples in a book they are reading.

> The activities discussed in this chapter are hands-on activities. Many of these same skills have been taught through worksheets and workbooks in the past. What is your opinion of worksheets and workbooks? Is there an advantage to hands-on learning over worksheets/workbooks? Is there a place for both? What do you think?

My Pile/Your Pile

In "my pile/your pile," the teacher writes down some words that the child already knows on 3 × 5 index cards. The teacher then adds a few words that the child is trying to learn. The teacher holds up the cards flash card style, and the child reads the words as quickly as possible. If the word is read correctly, it goes in the child's pile.

If not, it goes in the teacher's pile, and the child is given another chance to read the word. The object is for the child to be able to read the stack very quickly. New words can be added as the child masters the stack. My pile/your pile helps with instant recognition of sight words.

All of these strategies help to strengthen children's use of the cueing systems, and they help them learn strategies that will enable them to become independent readers. These strategies can be used with students of any age. They can be taught through mini-lessons, as a whole group, small group, or individually. We want to keep trying everything until we find out what works for each individual child.

Let's look now at some phonics applications. Single letters are either vowels or consonants. The vowels are a, e, i, o, and u. The consonants are a, b, c, d, f, g, h, j, k, l, m, n, p, q, r, s, t, v, w, x, y, and z. In some cases, y can be a vowel, as in the words "fly" and "pony." Short vowels are marked with a breve (ŭ), and long vowels are marked with a macron (ū).

In addition to vowels and consonants, there are also vowel digraphs, consonant digraphs, diphthongs, blends, r-controlled vowels, and the schwa sound. Vowel digraphs are vowel clusters that make one sound, like ea, oa, ou, ei, etc.

Some words with vowel digraphs are eat, teach, group, boat, and either. Consonant digraphs are consonant clusters that make one sound, like ph, sh, ch, gh, etc. Some words with consonant digraphs include phone, ship, chop, and graph.

Diphthongs are vowel clusters that go from one vowel sound to another within the same syllable, like oy, oi, ow. Some words with diphthongs include joy, oil, and how.

An r-controlled vowel is a vowel that is changed by the "r" sound, like ir, ar, ur, or, and er. Some words with an r-controlled vowel are first, art, hurt, organ, and teacher. A schwa is the vowel sound in an unaccented syllable. It usually makes the "uh" sound. Words with a schwa sound include, Melinda (both the e and the a), pencil (the i), and zebra (the a).

One big thing to remember about phonics is that it should be taught within the context of reading and writing, rather than in isolation. Teaching phonics within reading and writing is much more meaningful for students than to teach it in isolation.

Vocabulary

Tompkins (2015) states, "Children's knowledge of words plays a tremendous role in comprehension because it's difficult to decode and comprehend a text that's loaded with unfamiliar words" (p. 218). Seidlitz and Perryman (2011) name two different types of academic vocabulary: brick and mortar words. According to the authors, brick words are specific to a certain content, and mortar words are used to support brick words, just as mortar holds bricks together. Mortar words are still academic words, and they "connect, describe, or help us process the Brick words" (p. 98). For example, second graders learning about planets might learn the brick terms "Mars," "Jupiter," "orbit," and "solar system." Some examples of mortar terms that might be used to talk about planets are "based upon," "similar," "represent," and "opinion." Brick terms can be taught in many ways, using personal dictionaries or other vocabulary strategies we will talk about next. Mortar words are best taught by modeling, repetition, and asking students to talk like a scientist or talk like a mathematician. For example, the teacher could ask first graders who have just made a real graph out of apples, "Based upon the graph, which color of apple has the greater number?" For second graders who have just read *Where the Wild Things Are* (Sendak, 1964), the teacher could ask, "What is your opinion of Max?" Students will become accustomed to using the mortar words the more they hear them. Teachers can provide sentence stems to support students, especially English learners, as they learn to use mortar words.

Marzano (2004) suggests using a six-step method for students to learn vocabulary. In the first step, the teacher describes the word and what it means in everyday language. Next, students describe the word in their own words. They can first tell it to a partner, then write it down on a foldable or in their notebook. Next, students draw a picture of the word on a foldable or in their notebook. The next step is "do" in which students examine the word and look for prefixes, suffixes, etc. They could also make a diagram with similar or related words or write the word in a sentence. The last step is "play," and students participate in some type of game using the word. It can be "go fish," the memory game (concentration) or any type of game you can think of.

Children should be surrounded by print in the classroom. It is helpful to label various items in the classroom, have posters with print, have students' work displayed in the room, and have reading and writing centers with plenty of books and paper available. Word walls are also very helpful to use to help students learn vocabulary. In a typical word all, there is a space on the wall with each letter of the alphabet, and as words are learned by the class, they are added under the appropriate letter. Students can use those words for a reference, or they can "Read the room," pointing to words on the word wall and other labels in the classroom and reading them.

Students can also keep a personal dictionary, which would be a notebook or composition book kept at students' workspaces. There are a few pages for each letter, and words are added as they are added to the word wall and as individual students learn new words. Seidlitz and Perryman (2011) state, "It doesn't matter which strategies we use as long as we remain focused on our goal: helping students develop a deep understanding of academic vocabulary so they can achieve in school and communicate in the real world" (p. 38).

Fluency

According to Tompkins (2015), fluency is "the ability to read quickly, accurately, and with expression" (p. 160). In order to become fluent readers, children must develop automaticity, speed, and prosody (Tompkins, 2015). Automaticity is the ability to recognize words automatically and decode unfamiliar words quickly, and prosody is reading with expression and phrasing. Teachers can help children develop reading fluency through modeling and guided and independent practice using a variety of familiar texts. Clay (1993) stated, "the practice of rereading familiar books encourages confidence and fluency" (p. 38). Familiar books can be kept in a basket on the child's workspace to be read over and over again.

One excellent way for students to practice rereading a text is to prepare to read a Readers Theater script. If children know they are preparing for a performance, they have an authentic reason for practicing the script (Rasinski, 2006). In Readers Theater, children practice a script several times, then perform it for an audience. Props or masks can be used, but they are not necessary. The point is for the child to reread the script several times in order to develop expression and phrasing. During the performance, the children read the script rather than memorize it. Premade scripts or teacher-made scripts can be used. After children have practiced doing Readers Theater many times, they can develop their own scripts from favorite books, or can create an original script. Researchers have determined that Readers Theater substantially improves students' fluency (Griffith & Rasinski, 2004; Martinez, Roser, & Strecker, 1999; Tompkins, 2010). In addition, Young, Stokes, & Rasinski (2017) suggest combining word study with Readers Theater by identifying and analyzing unknown and interesting words, adding them to the word wall, and identifying roots and affixes. In addition, the authors talk about improving comprehension by asking questions about the script, writing a summary of the script, talking about the meaning of the script, and retelling the script to a partner.

Children can also participate in radio reading (Greene, 1979; Opitz & Rasinski, 1998; Searfoss, 1975) to improve fluency. Radio reading is done by first reading a text silently. Then the teacher assigns parts of the text to individual children, who practice reading the text aloud on their own. The next day, students get into groups and read their text together, as if they are professional actors or announcers (Cox, Miller, & Berg, 2013). The class then has a whole group discussion over comments and questions that groups have about the reading (Rasinski, 2003).

Another authentic way for students to practice rereading is to have a poetry café (Cox et al., 2013). Students choose a poem to read for the café, and practice throughout the week. On the day of the Poetry Café, each student reads their poem aloud for the group, and usually soft music plays in the background and refreshments can be served. Repeated reading can not only improve children's reading fluency, but it can increase word recognition, comprehension, and reading performance. (Cox et al., 2013; Rasinski, 2003; Tompkins, 2010).

Comprehension

Comprehension is the part of reading that involves constructing meaning by interacting with the text. Meaning-making is the goal of reading, so comprehension is extremely important to reading. Teachers can help students make connections to the reading by activating their background knowledge (Tompkins, 2015). Each child brings something different to the text, depending upon their background knowledge and lived experiences. According to Zimmerman and Hutchins (2003), "the meaning you get from a piece is intertwined with the meaning you bring to it" (p. 45). For instance, if children are going to read a book about the zoo, the teacher could bring in pictures or videos of zoo animals or toy zoo animals to introduce the book. Children who have been to the zoo before will likely make connections right away. Those who have not will be able to make connections by looking at the pictures and talking about them. The teacher can further help students make connections by giving a book introduction and talking with the children about pictures and known and unknown words in the text. Book introductions help children know what to expect from a text.

Students can also make predictions about what is going to happen next in the text based upon their past experiences and what they know about stories. It is good to use predictable texts with emergent readers, as the more students can predict and make sense of what is happening in the story, the more meaning they will get from the story. Predictable books typically have a pattern that repeats itself on each page, such as "Tommy goes to the beach, and his dog comes along. Tommy goes to the park, and his dog comes along, etc."

As students are reading a text, teachers can use prompts to guide them to think about what makes sense, and what they know about stories. The students are learning to use visual (graphophonic), structural (syntactic), and meaning (semantic) cues as they read, and the teacher can use prompts, such as "What do you think it could be?" or "What would make sense there?" to help them with comprehension.

Children can also monitor their understanding of a text and ask themselves questions as they read (Tompkins, 2015). Teachers can model this internal conversation through think-alouds and read-alouds. The more practice students get at reading, the more they will learn to use comprehension strategies and create meaning from the text.

Literacy Centers

Literacy centers provide constructive ways for students to work independently or in small groups to practice skills they have already been taught (Seefeldt & Galper, 2006). Teachers can model expectations for procedures for use of the centers, and they can be role-played and practiced to ensure students can work independently (Tompkins, 2003). Students can work on various literacy activities that provide meaningful practice on skills and strategies they are learning. Possible centers could include listening/viewing; any content—math, science, social studies; folder activities or game centers; manipulatives—magnetic letters; puzzles, or playdough or shaving cream for making letters or numbers; and reading—buddy reading, reading to a teddy bear, or word-sorting activities. Centers can be changed frequently to make sure to keep children's interest.

In a balanced literacy classroom, it is important to have a good balance between learning how to read and write and practicing reading and writing. The strategies and word work discussed in this chapter are excellent ways to support students with engaging, hands-on activities as they are learning to read and write, and they can be done as a part of Reading and Writing workshops.

References

Armbruster, B. B., Lehr, F., & Osborn, J. (2001). *Put reading first: The research building blocks for teaching children to read.* Urbana, IL: Center for the Improvement of Early Reading Achievement.

Bear, D., Invernizzi, M., Templeton, S., & Johnston, F. (2004). *Words their way: Word study for phonics, vocabulary, and spelling instruction.* Upper Saddle River, NJ: Pearson Merrill Prentice Hall.

Clay, M. (1993). *Reading recovery: A guidebook for teachers in training.* Auckland: Heinemann.

Cox, D., Miller, M., & Berg, H. (2013). Getting my nervouses out: The power of repeated oral reading performance to develop fluency in bilingual readers. *The Journal of Multiculturalism in Education, 8.*

Greene, F. (1979). Radio reading. In C. Pennock (Ed.), *Reading comprehension at four linguistic levels* (pp. 104–107). Newark, NJ: International Reading Association.

Gonzalez, V., & Miller, M. (2020). *Reading and writing with English learners.* San Clemente CA: Seidlitz Education.

Griffith, L. W., & Rasinski, T. V. (2004). A focus on fluency: How one teacher incorporated fluency with her reading curriculum. *The Reading Teacher, 58,* 126–137.

Martinez, M., Roser, N., & Strecker, S. (1999). I never thought I could be a star: A Readers Theatre ticket to fluency. *The Reading Teacher, 52,* 326–333.

Marzano, R. (2004). *Building background knowledge for academic achievement: Research on what works in schools.* Alexandria, VA: ASCD.

Opitz, M., & Rasinski, T. (1998). *Good-bye Round Robin: 25 Effective oral reading strategies.* Portsmouth, NH: Heinemann.

Pinnell, G., & Fountas, I. (1998). *Word matters: Teaching phonics and spelling in the reading/writing classroom.* Portsmouth, NH: Heinemann.

Rasinski, T. (2003). *The fluent reader.* New York: Scholastic Professional Books. (Original work published, 1989).

Rasinski, T. (2006). Fluency: An oft-neglected goal of the reading program. In C. Cummins (Ed.), *Understanding and implementing reading first initiatives: The changing role of administrators* (pp. 60–71). Newark, DE: International Reading Association.

Searfoss, L. (1975). Radio reading. *The reading teacher, 29,* 295–296.

Seefeldt, C., & Galper, A. (2006). *Active experiences for active children.* New York: Pearson.

Seidlitz, J., & Perryman, B. (2011). *7 Steps to a language-rich interactive classroom: Research-based strategies for engaging all students.* San Clemente, CA: Seidlitz Education.

Sendak, M. (1964). *Where the wild things are.* New York: Harper & Row.

Shaw, N. (1986). *Sheep in a jeep.* New York: Houghton Mifflin.

Tompkins, G. (2015). *Literacy in the early grades: A successful start for PreK-4 readers and writers.* Boston, MA: Pearson.

Tompkins, G. E. (2003). Literacy for the 21st century (3rd ed.). Upper Saddle River, NJ: Pearson Education.

Tompkins, G. E. (2010). *Literacy for the 21st Century: A balanced approach* (5th ed.). Boston, MA: Allyn & Bacon.

Young, C., Stokes, F., & Rasinski, T. (2017). Readers theater plus comprehension and word study. *The Reading Teacher, 71 (3).*

Zimmerman, S., & Hutchins, C. (2003). *7 Keys to comprehension.* New York: Three Rivers Press.

CHAPTER 5

Reading Workshop

Mr. Johnson reads aloud The Day Jimmy's Boa Ate the Wash, *then leads his second graders in a mini-lesson on reading strategies to use if you get stuck on a word. He passed out little bookmarks for students to write on, and they wrote down strategies as the class discussed them. With Mr. Johnson's help, the students named these strategies to write on their bookmarks: "re-read, check the picture, think about what makes sense, try the word and read past it, think of another word that looks like that word, and think about the sounds in the word." After the students have written down their strategies, Mr. Johnson sends them off to find a spot to read for Drop Everything and Read (DEAR) time. He reminds them to look at the strategies on their bookmarks if they get stuck on a word while they are reading. Students excitedly scatter about the room and snuggle up with pillows and sprawl on beanbag chairs. Mr. Johnson sets the timer for 20 minutes, and students begin to read. When the timer goes off, students go back to their seats, and Mr. Johnson reminds them that they can continue to read, or they may begin their book projects if they have finished their book. He quickly goes over the literacy centers that students may use if they are finished making their book projects. Several students go to the crafts area and begin to plan the project they will make to share their books. Others continue to read. Mr. Johnson calls three different students to come and have a reading conference, then he calls a group to come for guided reading. Finally, when time is almost up for Reading Workshop, Mr. Johnson asks how many students are ready to share their book projects. Three students raise their hands, and Mr. Johnson asks all students to come to the carpet for sharing time. Samuel shares a mobile he made showing the characters, setting, and plot of his story. Juan does a puppet show about his book, using paper bag puppets he made. Benita has rewritten the book If You Give a Mouse a Cookie (Numeroff, 1985) as "If You Give a Dog a Bone." Students listen eagerly as their classmates share, and they clap and compliment them when they are finished. After everyone has shared, Mr. Johnson asks them to go get their lunch boxes and line up for lunch.*

I can remember a time when reading instruction revolved around basal readers, and instruction focused on the teacher's guide that went with the basal series. Reading instruction was basically one-size-fits-all and did not take individual needs into consideration. Children read aloud "round robin" style in their reading groups, and typically, teachers would ask questions from the teacher's guide at the end of the story. Atwell (1987) wrote about Reading Workshop in 1987. Reading Workshop is individualized, and children are able to have sustained time to read books of their choice independently. Teachers explicitly teach mini-lessons based upon students' reading needs during workshop time. In addition, students respond to what they have read through writing, conversations, and reading projects based upon their books.

According to Ken Goodman, the classroom should be a literate environment in which the printed word is everywhere (Goodman, 1986). This type of atmosphere fosters literacy development, as well as instilling a love of reading and writing in the learner. In addition, readers need to have an extended time to read every day, choice of what they will read, and a way to respond to what they have read. Templeton and Gehsmann (2014) state that children are more motivated to read when they are able to choose books in which they are interested that are at their reading level for independent reading time. Reading Workshop fits naturally into the balanced literacy environment and helps to meet the needs of the children as literacy learners. In Reading Workshop, children have the opportunity to work individually at their own level and at their own pace with literature they have chosen. In addition, readers have a daily sustained time to read, and they have many opportunities to respond to what they have read. Teachers implement some or all of the following components within reading workshops to meet students' individual needs: sustained silent reading (independent reading time), reader response journals, teacher–student conferences, guided reading, literature circles, literacy centers, literature extensions, shared book experiences, read-aloud time, and mini-lessons.

Reading Mini-Lessons

Atwell (1987) begins her reading workshop with a mini-lesson, spending 5 minutes talking about an author or a genre, or she reads and discusses a poem or a short story. Templeton (1995) describes mini-lessons as "direct teaching that occurs in an authentic literacy context: we teach a particular skill to particular students when we perceive that those students need that skill" (p. 263).

Teachers can introduce the procedures for Reading Workshop in a mini-lesson. Students can role-play and practice the procedures and discuss expectations before working individually. During mini-lessons, teachers can also address how to choose books for reading independently. In addition, teachers can do mini-lessons on word identification strategies and comprehension strategies they can use as they are reading independently (Tompkins, 2014).

Some teachers do both a mini-lesson and a read-aloud. They might read a picture book, a poem, or a chapter of a chapter book. Trelease (1985) states that reading aloud to children helps them to grow in terms of emotional development, and helps to expand their imagination and develop language. In addition, teachers serve as a model of fluent reading as they read aloud, and they can read books that are above students' reading level that they can still comprehend.

Independent Reading Time

After the mini-lesson and/or read-aloud, students have an independent reading time. Depending upon the grade level of students, this time lasts from 15 to 30 minutes, generally. Norton (1992) describes uninterrupted sustained silent reading, "USSR," as being a specified time when everyone takes out a book and reads, including the teacher, to serve as a model (Norton, 1992). Some teachers refer to this time as "Drop Everything and Read (DEAR)" time (Templeton & Gehsmann, 2014). Gallagher (2009) states that sustained silent reading "is necessary to allow students to build their prior knowledge and background" (p. 43). The author also notes that it helps students learn to read for pleasure. Norton stresses that "enjoyment is emphasized because students are not expected or even permitted to read other types of assignments during this time" (p. 29). Students are typically able to sit on beanbag chairs or lean on pillows as they read. I used to have a reading bathtub where students could take turns sitting with pillows to read, and I let a different student sit at my desk every day during this time. In other classrooms, I have seen couches where students could read. Daily time for sustained, silent reading of self-selected books is important in order for children to develop fluency in reading and to develop an enjoyment of reading. Atwell (1987) states, ". . . we know readers' fluency is a function of sustained experiences with printed texts," (p. 156) and she recommends that children have a sustained, silent reading time daily. "I've learned to make time for real reading," she states, and "periods of silent, independent reading are perhaps the strongest experience I can provide students to demonstrate the value of literacy" (p. 157). In addition, Templeton and Gehsmann (2014) state that daily reading practice is necessary in order for children to develop fluency in reading.

Atwell (1987) also stresses the importance of children's ownership over their reading, and states that they should be allowed to select books they are interested in reading. When children are allowed a choice in reading material, they feel motivated to read and to develop an appreciation for literature. She further states that "allowing readers to choose also helps their fluency," and "I heard again and again from readers of every ability that freedom of choice had increased both reading rate and comprehension" (p. 162).

According to Butler and Turbill (1986), "Every day, adequate time must be provided for the children to practice the processes of reading and writing. They need time to think about, and talk about their reading and writing, and need to know that there will be time to continue any unfinished writing or reading task at the next language period (p. 22)." They go on to state that children should have the choice of what to read or write about and that "these choices will stem mainly from their own experiences and interests" (p. 22).

"Development in reading and writing can only take place in an environment where students regularly engage in reading and writing, where there are frequent opportunities for students to read and write whole, meaningful texts," state Rhodes and Dudley-Marling (1988, p. 80). They also suggest that reading should "permeate the day" (p. 81).

Responding to Text

According to Tompkins (2014), "Students respond to what they have read and continue to negotiate the meaning after reading" (p. 45). Students can respond to a text through reading response journals, literature extension activities, and through reading conferences. Miller (2009) states, "Students should respond in natural ways to the books they are reading through conferences, written entries, classroom discussions, and projects" (p. 16). A reading response journal is a record of the books a child has read, initial impressions of books, and reactions to the books after the reading. Response logs can include a written response in the form of a dialogue between the teacher and the student (or between two students) about the literature (Tompkins, 2015). According to Tompkins, "Responses often demonstrate children's reading strategies and offer insights into their thinking about literature; seeing how children think about their reading helps teachers guide their learning" (p. 306). Atwell (1987) describes how she and her husband and friends often sit around the dining room table discussing literature, authors, and ideas. She discovered that reading response journals provides a similar experience for all of her students.

Atwell describes response journals as "reflecting on reading" and "extending and enriching reflection through collaboration" (p. 165). The response journal can be written or typed, or can even be done in the form of a blog. According to Routman (1988), "a look into a reading log or reading spiral demonstrates the child's written ability to synthesize and interpret information from silent reading and oral discussion, as well as give an opinion about the book" (p. 206). She explains that response journals can be used to make predictions about the text before reading, summarize a story, or give a personal opinion about a certain piece of literature.

According to Routman (1988), the response journal fits nicely with discussion groups, or literature circles, which are small groups that meet on a regular basis to discuss books that the group members have read. Students can draw from what they have written in their response journals to guide the discussion. Literature circles and literature discussion groups improve listening skills and comprehension, and they enable English learners or struggling readers to succeed as they observe the more proficient readers, and as they slowly begin to participate more and more in the discussions and write more and more in their response logs (Routman, 1988). You can encourage participation by providing sentence stems for students, such as "My favorite part of the book was _____, I thought the character _____, etc." Sentence stems provide access to academic language for English Learners and struggling readers (Seidlitz, 2019).

Another way for a child to respond to literature is through literature extension activities, such as writing inspired by a story, a retelling of the story, artwork inspired by the story, rewriting the ending of a story, making story maps, making a mural, listening to the story on tape, creating a tape of an oral reading of the story, or a puppet show or play depicting the story. My second graders loved to present plays and puppet shows about their reading. They also did what they called a "shadow play," which was done by cutting out shapes of characters in the story, placing them on the overhead projector, and acting out the story. This can also be done by using a doc camera. Routman (1988) states "an important part of our language arts program are the activities that extend and complement the literature, as well as those that examine the literature more closely" (p. 67). Routman stresses the importance of allowing children to respond to literature through art, drama, and music in order to convey their interpretations of the literature (Routman, 1988).

Routman further describes literature extensions as any "meaningful extension of a favorite book, especially if it requires the child to reexamine the text and the illustrations" (Routman, 1988, p. 67). Literature can also be extended by reading additional books that compare to the original book in terms of genre, point of view, or story structure (Norton, 1992). In addition, Templeton and Gehsmann (2014) recommend that students role-play, draw, or write about something they have read in an informational text.

Conferences

While students are working individually on projects, literature circles, literacy centers, or reading, the teacher calls students for reading conferences. Teacher–student reading conferences also allow students to respond to what they have read. In a reading conference, the teacher and the student meet one-on-one, and the student is asked to retell a self-selected story and read a portion of it orally. Typically, a teacher will then ask open-ended or thought-provoking questions, as well as literal and recall questions. Many teachers also do running records during conferences to monitor students' progress.

According to Butler and Turbill (1986), reading conferences enable a teacher to "assess such things as levels of reading comprehension, and ability to read critically, as well as the capacity to form opinions about what has been read" (p. 50). The conference also enables a teacher to "ascertain a child's reading needs and interests, and attitudes to reading in general" (p. 50). Rhodes and Dudley-Marling (1988) state that a reading conference is "a natural part of teaching reading" when it is viewed as an opportunity for the reader to benefit from sharing what is being read (p. 128).

Sharing Time

At the end of Reading Workshop time, many teachers have students gather to share about what they read (Tompkins, 2015). Templeton and Gehsmann (2014) suggest giving students a prompt, such as "Take a moment to think about what you learned about yourself as a reader today or this week" (p. 93). This is a time for students to reflect on their learning, according to the authors, as well as "a time when students can learn from each other; (which) is often the richest learning of all" (p. 93). Sharing time is also the time when students share their written response or artistic response to what they have read. I always had my students sign up when they were ready to share. We sat in a big circle on the floor while students stood at their spot in the circle to share their project. Many times, students did puppet shows or recruited others to help them present a play at this time. All students are able to share their response to their reading or the project they made, no matter what reading level they are on. Participating in sharing time gives struggling readers and English learners confidence when they are able to participate the same as everyone else. Tompkins tells us that "Sharing is important because it helps students become a classroom community to value and celebrate each other's accomplishments" (p. 352).

Finding the Right Book

We have talked about how it is important for students to have a choice of what to read. It is equally important that they find the right book to read, in order to become hooked on reading. Templeton and Gehsmann state that, "Just-right books are texts your students can read with high levels of comprehension and accuracy" (p. 91). For independent reading time, students should be reading books they can read with 95% to 100% accuracy. Ohlhausen and Jepsen (1992) recommend what they call "The Goldilocks Strategy" for students to use when choosing books. They categorize books as "Too Easy," "Just Right," or "Too Hard." "Too-Easy" books are familiar books that can be read fluently, for the most part. "Too-Hard" books are those above a student's reading level that cannot be read without significant miscues and breakdown of meaning. "Just-Right" books are those that interest the reader and contain very few unfamiliar words. The child is able to read a "Just-Right" book independently using their sight words and reading strategies.

When students choose a book that is too difficult for them to read, the authors suggest giving them instruction or a book introduction to scaffold their understanding, suggesting they choose another book, or letting them problem solve in order to try and read the book. Most likely, if they are not able to read the book, they will decide to choose another book. You can gently suggest that if a book is mostly confusing, it is probably not their just-right book. Especially, students who struggle may find it difficult to find the right book, as there may not be books on their level that also match their interests. You can help these students out by providing high-interest books at lower levels, by giving them a choice of a few books on their level, or giving book talks on lower-level books to entice students to read them (Templeton & Gehsmann, 2014). Giving a book talk may also make these lower-level choices more "socially acceptable" (p. 92).

Reading Workshop not only provides students with time, choice, and response to their reading, but it places them in a print-rich environment that supports them as they develop as readers. Teachers are able to cater to individual needs through conferences and mini-lessons, and students are able to work at their own pace and their own level. Students work in a low-stress environment as a community of learners who support and celebrate each other as they learn literacy.

> What are some ways you could create a print-rich environment? What are some of the things you would choose? What types of books and materials would you have?

References

Atwell, N. (1987). *In the middle: Writing, reading, and learning with adolescents.* Portsmouth, NH: Heinemann.

Butler, A., & Turbill, J. (1986). *Towards a reading-writing classroom.* Australia: Primary English Teaching Association.

Gallagher, K. (2009). *Readicide: How schools are killing reading and what you can do about it.* Portland, ME: Stenhouse Publishers.

Goodman, K. S. (1986). *What's whole in whole language?* Portsmouth, NH: Heinemann.

Miller, D. (2009). *The book whisperer: Awakening the inner reader in every child.* San Francisco, CA: Jossey-Bass.

Norton, D. (1992). *The impact of literature-based reading.* New York: Merrill.

Numeroff, L. (1985). *If you give a mouse a cookie.* New York: Harper Collins.

Ohlhausen, M. M., & Jepsen, M. (1992). Lessons from Goldilocks: "Somebody's been choosing my books, but I can make my own choices now!" *The New Advocate, 5,* 31–46.

Rhodes, L., & Dudley-Marling, C. (1988). *Readers and writers with a difference: A holistic approach to teaching learning disabled and remedial students.* Portsmouth, NH: Heinemann.

Routman, R. (1988). *Transitions: From literature to literacy.* Portsmouth, NH: Heinemann.

Seidlitz, J. (2019). *Sheltered instruction in Texas: Second language acquisition methods for teachers of ELs.* Irving, TX: Seidlitz Education.

Templeton, S. (1995). *Children's literacy: Contexts for meaningful learning.* Geneva, IL: Houghton Mifflin Company.

Templeton, S., & Gehsmann, K. (2014). *Teaching reading and writing: The developmental approach.* Boston, MA: Pearson.

Tompkins, G. (2014). *Literacy for the 21st century: A balanced approach.* Boston, MA: Pearson.

Tompkins, G. (2015). *Literacy in the early grades: A successful start for Pre-K-4 readers and writers.* Boston: Pearson.

Trelease, J. (1985). *The read-aloud handbook.* New York: Penguin Books.

CHAPTER 6

Writing Workshop

Ms. Garcia passed golf pencils out to her second graders and asked them to get out a sheet of paper. Next, she asked them to make a list of things they might want to write about. She gave them several minutes to make their list, then she instructed them to draw a circle around the topic they wanted to write about the most. She then told them that this is what they would write about first. She next demonstrated how to make a web for thinking about what they would write. She gave an example of a topic, "cats" and wrote the word on the whiteboard and circled it. Then she made five other circles and then drew lines to the main circle and did a think-aloud as she wrote different things about cats in each circle. Next, she asked the students to do the same thing with their topic. After all students had made their webs, she asked them to share them with their shoulder partners. She then told the students she was going to start her writing piece about cats, and she did a write-aloud as she wrote. Ms. Garcia asked the students to talk to their shoulder partner about what she did when she wrote her piece, then they read what she had written chorally. After that, she told them to start their writing pieces. After about 15 minutes, she asked them to read what they had written to their shoulder partner. Next, she passed out folders and said, "This is your writing folder, and you will keep your writing piece and your web in your folder. Tomorrow, we will continue with the writing process, and we will make some changes to what you have written. When you finish your pieces, we are going to make them into books." The children placed their writing pieces and webs in their folders, chattering excitedly about making books. Ms. Garcia picked up the folders and placed them in a tub on the window sill.

I have always been a writer, and I have always felt a sense of excitement as I sit down to think about what I want to write. As the writing begins to flow, I feel joy. My friend and colleague, Hannah Gerber, once said that she feels as if her words are "dancing across the page," as she writes. That sums it up. That is a great way to say it. At school in first grade, I was given writing assignments that required correct spelling, best handwriting, and a limited space in which to write at the bottom of a page where there was space for a picture at the top. Since everything had to be correct, I remember using only words I knew how to spell. If I did misspell something, I remember erasing and the thin paper tearing and smearing with pencil smudges. I couldn't wait to get home and write with my second grade sister in our composition books our dad had given us. We wrote about whatever we wanted to write about, and we had as much time to write as we wanted. We talked excitedly as we planned and wrote our books, using invented spelling, or occasionally asking our parents how to spell words. We wrote about what we knew and loved—our cats and their kittens. We read what we had written to each other, to our parents, to our friends, and to our grandparents when they came to visit. That was a time of pure joy, and I want every child to feel that kind of delight and happiness as they create beautiful masterpieces about their lived experiences.

According to Fletcher and Portalupi (2001), "It is crucial for students to have frequent, predictable time set aside for them to write" (p. 8). They recommend students write at least three days each week, though four or five days per week would be the best. The authors go on to state that choice is an important factor in students' writing. Writers must have an authentic reason to write, and they "know best which topics and purposes for writing matter most to each of them" (p. 10). Graves (1983) tells us that when students are able to choose their own topics, they make greater strides in their writing development. He states, with topic choice, "the child exercises strongest control, establishes ownership, and with ownership, pride in the piece" (p. 21). In addition to time, and choice, writers also need response to their writing (Fletcher & Portalupi, 2001). Calkins and Ehrenworth (2016) agree that young writers need a scheduled time to write, choice of what to write about, and response to their writing from teachers and peers. For me, all of this occurred organically at home. We can replicate that environment for our students with Writer's Workshop. Writer's Workshop provides writers with these needs: sustained time to write, choice in what they will write about, and response to their writing through conferences and sharing time.

In Writer's Workshop, students go through the writing process with a topic of their choice. The writing process includes prewriting, drafting, revising, editing, and publishing. The editing and revising steps do not need to be in a certain order, and revising and editing can also occur naturally in the drafting stage for more advanced writers. Cooper (2000) recommends posting the steps of the writing process on a poster so students can refer to it.

A typical writer's workshop might follow the following format: mini-lesson, status of the class, independent writing time (the time they are working on various stages of the writing process), writing conferences (with teacher and peers), and sharing time.

Writing Mini-Lessons

Writing mini-lessons can be a time to demonstrate the writing process, a specific skill involved in writing, or a new genre of writing. It is necessary for the teacher to walk students through the writing process, as Ms. Garcia did in the scenario, through modeling, think-aloud, and write-aloud. Especially for young children, the writing process may need to be done as a group a few times before students do it on their own. They need to learn expectations and procedures before they do the process independently.

Many teachers share literature during writing mini-lessons in order to show students examples of techniques used by authors. *What you know first* (MacLachlan, 1998) has excellent examples of imagery, and *Night in the Country* (Rylant, 1986), has many onomatopoeias and other vivid words throughout the text. Fletcher and Portalupi (2001) stress that the book should be familiar to students before using it in a writing mini-lesson, so they can focus on the writer's craft, rather than the story. The authors have also used literature to show different purposes for writing and different ways they can make readers have different reactions to the text. In addition, they state, "We've used books to show how authors can write about the same topic but from the perspective of different genres" (p. 81).

Status of the Class

After the mini-lesson, teachers typically keep track of where students are within the writing process through a status of the class report. A chart can be used with all the students' names on the side and dates going across the top. You can use a coding system to note each part of the writing process so you can mark that for each child. For instance, for prewriting, you could mark down a "p," for drafting, you could mark a "d," etc. Status of the class not only holds students responsible for working on a specific part of the writing process, but it helps them organize and plan their writing piece.

Independent Writing Time

Independent writing time is when students work on the various steps of the writing process, and it should be an uninterrupted time. First, students choose a topic, as in the scenario. They can keep a list of possible topics in their writing folder and add to the list as they think of something new to write about. It is important for children to write about things they know about and things they like, which will help them to be more engaged in the writing process (Tompkins, 2014). For children having trouble finding something to write about, the teacher can sit beside them and demonstrate the process of choosing a topic again. Children come to school with many different experiences, and if you can get them to talk about what they like to do at home, who they play with, or even what they like to eat, they will realize they have a lot to write about.

Prewriting is the time students plan out and organize their writing by choosing a topic and brainstorming ideas. According to Cooper (2000), students should "consider the purpose for their writing and the audience for whom they are writing" (p. 353). This process should be modeled for students through a write-aloud. According to Tompkins (2014), many teachers do not spend enough time on prewriting, though it is a very important part of the writing process. In fact, Murray (1982) stresses that 70% of the writing process should be spent on prewriting.

When it is time for students to begin drafting, the teacher can do another write-aloud to model the process for the class. This may need to be done several times while students learn to use the writing process. Cooper (2000) suggests having students use either lined or plain white paper for drafting and skip a line after every line to leave a space for revising. He states, "This practice helps them develop a positive attitude toward revision; it lets them know that changes can and will be made and that it is all right to make changes in their writing" (p. 353). Tompkins (2014) reminds us to make sure students write on only one side of the paper so they will be able to cut their draft apart as they revise. Teachers should accept any form of writing and stress to students that they are writing their first draft. For very young students, their drafting will likely be done with drawings and some letters or words used as labels. Students should be encouraged to get their thoughts down on the paper, and you can assure them they will have plenty of time to make corrections during revision. That is why Ms. Garcia used the golf pencils. Because they have no erasers, students will not be tempted to erase something they are unsure of. Cooper tells us, "…the object is for students to express their ideas freely and creatively; they should not be hampered by worrying about spelling" (p. 357).

While students are drafting, you can encourage them to spell things the best they can by saying the words, listening to the sounds, and writing down the letters, using invented spelling. Children need to hear, however, that they will have plenty of time to go back and fix up the spellings and change or add to their first draft. Some teachers call the first draft the "sloppy copy" so students will be comfortable with adding to and changing it. Tompkins says, "Their drafts are usually messy, reflecting the outpouring of ideas with cross-outs, lines, and arrows as they think of better ways to express ideas" (p. 50). Some of my second graders took relish in making their sloppy copy look as messy as possible!

Revising is the next step of the writing process. Avery (2002) states, "Preparing writing for publication requires students to reread and rethink the piece and to make changes that refine the piece for their audience" (p. 203). Tompkins (2014) tells us that during the revision step, students are able to resee their writing pieces through the eyes of their teacher and peers. Another mini-lesson can be done to teach students how to revise and edit. Just as with prewriting and drafting, the teacher can do a write-aloud with their own writing piece to show the process of making revisions. One thing you can talk about is adding interesting words to replace ordinary words. Some teachers call these words "sparkle words." You could also talk about rereading to make sure your piece makes sense and rearranging sentences to make the piece sound better. Painter (2006) refers to revision as "the work that goes into saying what you want to say in the best possible way" (p. 31).

Cooper (2000) recommends teaching children to ask themselves these questions during the revision process: "1) Have I expressed my ideas clearly so that my audience will understand what I am saying? 2) Are there other ideas that I should add to my writing? 3) Are there other words that I can use to make my writing more exciting and interesting? 4) Are there better ways I can express my ideas?" (p. 359). He suggests posting these questions for students to refer to as they are revising.

After students have revised their writing pieces, they are ready to edit. According to Tompkins (2014), in the editing phase, students shift from focusing on content to concentrating on mechanics—spelling punctuation, capitalization, sentence structure, etc. Painter (2006) suggests teaching mini-lessons that will help students "understand the impact editing has on one's writing" (p. 106). To teach students how to edit their pieces, it is a good idea to model the process using your own writing piece, once again. A great place to start is to show students how they can go through their pieces and circle all the words they think might be misspelled. Next, you can show them how you can underline each sentence to make sure each sentence has a capital letter at the beginning and punctuation at the end. These, of course, would be previously taught through mini-lessons and practiced in literacy centers. Editing becomes more complex as students develop more and more writing proficiency, and the teacher can judge what students need to be held accountable for, based upon individual differences. Cooper (2000) suggests developing checklists with the students that show what to look for when editing, as they become more proficient writers. Editing for "commonly accepted conventions," according to Tompkins, "is a courtesy to those who will read the composition" (p. 53).

One important thing to remember when teaching editing is that young children may not realize when they have misspellings. I would suggest only having them correct words they have circled as being misspelled. Graves (1983) states that as children compose using invented spelling, they are using a similar process as when they learned to speak. They hear sounds and make approximations of what they hear on the page, and "letters run together as they do in speaking" (p. 184). Invented spelling is like a window into the child's brain, as it shows us what is going on inside their head as they are writing. Being able to think about the sounds and record them as words is a very complex skill. If children are not allowed to go through this process, it is more difficult for them to learn to write and spell. Avery (2002) states, "Invented spelling is not an excuse to be careless but rather an invitation to use knowledge of phonics, patterns, and structures and to *think* about spelling and to spell words the best way possible" (p. 366).

> Invented spelling can actually be a controversial topic. Teachers and parents alike disagree about whether or not children's writing should be displayed on the wall or sent home when all words are not spelled conventionally. Some teachers make sure everything is spelled correctly before a writing piece can be displayed on the wall or in the hall, and certainly if it is going home. Other teachers tell students to spell the best they can, perhaps correct two or three words students have identified as being misspelled, and post them or send them home with invented spelling. As you can imagine, parents have two types of reactions to the invented spelling. Some parents admire the writing and excitedly praise their children. Others come to the school demanding to know why their child isn't being taught spelling. What do you think? Which parents and teachers do you agree with?

According to Tompkins (2014), "Students bring their compositions to life by writing final copies and sharing them orally with an appropriate audience" (p. 55). Routman (2000) states, "Publishing (bringing a piece of writing to finished form) for real reasons and actual audiences motivates students to do their best writing" (p. 322). Cooper (2000) states, "This phase of the writing process authenticates the reason for writing and gives students pride and enjoyment in their own work" (p. 361). Children can publish their pieces in many different ways. They can type it up on the computer and illustrate it; or they can make a book with construction paper covers, illustrate it, laminate it, and put it together using a book binding machine. Book covers can also be made from manila folders. Tompkins describes booklets made by folding paper into halves or quarters with the title on the front and the composition on the other three pages. She also recommends making a cover for the book with wallpaper samples. These can be obtained by going to a store that sells wallpaper and asking for old sample books.

Another idea is to publish by writing in a composition book in their best handwriting, then illustrate. Students can even make their book into a shape book. They can cut out a cover from construction paper in a certain shape, then cut notebook paper in the same shape and staple it together. I have found that making a pattern to draw around from cardboard or an old manila folder works nicely for making sure pages are the same shape and size. Some examples of shape books might be a book in the shape of a dinosaur for a book about dinosaurs, or a book in the shape of a house for a book about a family.

Whichever way students publish their books, they can be very personalized and unique. My students used to love to have a dedication page and an "about the author" page, complete with a photo. Marsh and Missy were so proud of their published books they brought home each year. We still have all of them, along with class books my students have made together, and even my cat book written in first grade. These are prized possessions! According to Cooper (2000), "The excitement and pleasure on the faces of students after producing their first book are almost indescribable!" (p. 362). Students see themselves as authors when they have published a book. Many teachers and librarians display students' published books for other students to read and check out. Cooper tells us that these books are frequently read and checked out more than any other book. He suggests making time once a week or so for students to go to the library for the purpose of reading student-made books and discussing them with their peers. This serves not only as a celebration of students' writing, but it can also motivate students to publish their own books and give them writing ideas.

Writer's Craft

Tompkins (2014) discusses introducing students to writer's craft through mini-lessons and conferences to help them think about the writing process. She describes writer's craft as "Specific techniques that writers use to capture readers' attention and convey meaning" (p. 57). Students learn about and apply the 6 + 1 Traits of Writing to ensure they have the best possible writing piece that includes sprinkles of writer's craft throughout. The 6 + 1 Traits are discussed further in Chapter 9, and they include ideas, organization, word choice, sentence fluency, conventions, and presentation.

Students think about their ideas during the prewriting and drafting stages. After they have chosen a topic and developed the idea further through brainstorming or creating a web, they choose a genre for their piece and make sure to focus on and develop their topic. They consider organization when drafting and again during revision. They make sure to have an introduction that grabs the reader's attention, and they make sure to have transitions that make sense, as well as a strong ending. Students also focus on word choice and sentence fluency during revision. Word choice brings the child's voice to the writing piece. While students are choosing just the right words to make their piece come alive, they concentrate on "painting a picture with words, choosing precise words, energizing writing with strong verbs, and playing with words" (Tompkins, 2014, p. 58). Sentence fluency involves the rhythm and flow of the piece, and students focus on using a variety of sentence types and lengths. They make sure the writing has a pleasing sound and flow as it is read-aloud.

During the editing stage of the writing process, students focus on conventions, which include spelling, capitalization, and punctuation. Finally, when students publish their pieces, they think about the best presentation for their piece. They choose the way they want to publish, they make illustrations, and make sure to use their best handwriting or type their piece.

According to Tompkins, when students use the 6 + 1 Traits, they "internalize what good writers do" (p. 59). She suggests reading several beautifully written texts to use as examples of writer's craft. Graves (1983) recommends reading a variety of literature for students to use as inspiration. He states, "Since they have a strong sense of story and drama, and have heard the rich voices in the writing, they have the urge to produce literature" (p. 29). Fletcher and Portalupi (2001) recommend that students keep a writer's notebook to jot down ideas for writing or beginnings of new pieces. Fletcher (1996) describes a writer's notebook as "a container to keep all the seeds you gather until you are ready to plant them" (p. 1).

He states, "It gives you a quiet place to catch your breath and begin to write" (p. 1). Students can keep their writer's notebook with them, and when they think of an idea of something to write about, they can write it down for later. They can jot down what they notice, what they find interesting, and beautiful words or phrases they hear. They can even include artifacts, sketches, drawings, or photos that will inspire them as they sit down to think, create, and compose the next piece.

Writing Conferences

While students are involved in independent writing, teachers can call individual students to bring their writing for a writing conference. According to Routman (2000), "Conferencing is an opportunity to listen, appreciate, affirm, respect, reinforce, suggest, and/or teach" (p. 309). It is also a time to celebrate the child's writing. Typically, the teacher will have the student start off by reading their piece, then ask questions about the content. If something is unclear, the teacher could say something like, "Here is what I am wondering about what you wrote . . ." then encourage them to revise in a way that makes sense or explains what they are talking about. Especially for younger children, it is sometimes hard for them to understand that the reader may not understand something because they don't have the same background knowledge as the child does. Asking questions such as this will help them realize that they need to add more information for the reader. In conferences, when students wanted to revise, I showed them how to write something that was to be added on strips of paper and tape them to the sides of the paper, making a note of where it should be inserted. If writing was to be rearranged, I encouraged them to cut the draft and tape it in a new order. Some of their sloppy copies turned out looking like spiders!

Fletcher and Portalupi (2001) suggest having editing conferences with students, and they encourage teachers to look for teachable moments in the students' editing. After reading the child's edited piece, teachers can identify skills and procedures on which a student may need some instruction. For example, if a student has used only simple sentences in their writing, you could show them how they can combine some of their sentences. In addition, the authors stress the importance of students rereading their pieces. In fact, they state, "Rereading is the glue that connects the stages of writing" (p. 69). When writers reread many times throughout the process, they can hear what needs to be changed, what might not sound right, or which part sounds really good! Eventually, students will anticipate questions a reader might have about their writing piece, and they will be able to ask themselves the questions and make changes to their writing (Fletcher & Portalupi, 2001).

Another way to do a writing conference is to wheel around in your chair for a roving conference. In this type of conference, it is typical for the teacher to pull up to a student's desk and ask, "How's it going?" Students can read portions of their piece or ask for help with the wording of a passage. This is a less formal type of conference, and it is a good way to visit with several students in a shorter amount of time. You can plan formal conferences for Monday through Thursday, then do roving conferences on Fridays. In my classroom, students had a designated day for a conference each week.

Students can also have peer conferences with one another. In a peer conference, students sit together and take turns reading their pieces, asking questions, and making suggestions. They can do peer conferencing during independent writing time as well. Hearing something from their classmates' perspective is very helpful to students as they make decisions about their writing pieces. Routman (2000) urges students to make positive comments, but she doesn't want peer conferences to include only compliments. She states, "Now after I'm satisfied that a child has received a few genuine, positive comments, I encourage students to make suggestions or state points of confusion without giving a mandatory compliment" (p. 309). Routman reminds us, however, that although peer conferences are valuable, we should make sure that we conference one-on-one with each student to give them our professional guidance with their writing piece.

Sharing Writing

To finish up a daily writing workshop, teachers typically have a time for students to share their writing. According to Avery (2002), sharing time "is a ritual to end the workshop just as the mini-lesson is the opening" (p. 170). Some teachers have a special author's chair (Cooper, 2000) for students to sit in as they share, and they have the other students sit in a circle or on the carpet in front of the author's chair. After the child reads their writing piece, students have a discussion about the writing. Students can share their writing at any stage of completion. It can be their rough draft, their published piece, or anywhere in between. I always had students sign up on a sheet of paper near the author's chair when they wanted to share. Routman (2000) recommends having students practice reading their piece before sharing time, so the reading will go smoothly.

It is a good idea to model and have students role-play how to make comments or ask questions about someone's writing piece. It is especially important to stress how to make positive statements, and where there are confusions, ask questions like, ". . . can you tell me more about . . .?" Students will become proficient at making comments and questioning with time and practice.

Routman (2000) suggests that sharing time can also be a good time to model how to participate in a peer conference. She states, "Sharing time functions as a whole-class conference, a time not only to share and celebrate but to teach, reinforce strategies, set goals, and move students' writing forward" (p. 310). Routman goes on to describe how she typically chooses students who have an example in their writing of something they have learned in mini-lesson, a vivid use of words, or another writing technique she wants all the students to see during sharing time.

Another fun way to share writing is for students to take their writing pieces to another classroom and pair up with those students to read to them. They can also go and read to the principal or librarian as a special privilege or on a rotating basis.

Painter (2006) recommends having a writing museum to share students' writing. It can be set up on tables, and students can walk around and read each other's writing pieces while soft music plays in the background. Students can even leave comments on a sheet of paper or sticky note. In addition, she suggests letting students bring their lunches to the classroom and having a writing lunch. Students take turns reading their pieces and making comments.

Students also enjoy sharing their published pieces at an author's celebration. The celebration can be done in the library or cafeteria, and students can make invitations to invite their parents, grandparents, the principal, special teachers, and siblings.

Students can make decorations to go around the room, and parents can volunteer to send refreshments. The students can sit at tables around the room with chairs for an audience. When guests arrive, they rotate around and listen to several different students read their pieces. One way to do it is to divide the class into two groups. One group can share for 30 minutes, then the second group can share for the next 30 minutes. This way, students are able to rotate with the guests and hear their classmates read. When everyone has read their pieces, the students and the guests can have refreshments. The author's celebration is an excellent culmination for the school year or semester.

Along with several family members, I had the privilege of going to Marsh and Missy's author's celebration's when they were in elementary school, and they were such exciting experiences for all of us. When Missy was in college and worked with a child and took them through the writing process, I again got to go to her author's celebration with her and her student. That was an amazing thing for me to see as well!

Graves (1983) talks about how children come to school excited to write after experimenting with writing at home whenever they had the opportunity. They draw and write with crayons, markers, pencils, sidewalk chalk—whatever they can get their hands on. They even sometimes write on walls and in books, like my Missy did. They are chomping at the bit to get their story down on paper! But when teachers put restrictions on writing, they kill the child's joy and stifle their creativity. I always think back to my smudged papers with holes in them when I was trying to meet my teacher's expectations. I was not happy about that writing experience and not proud of what I had written. Writing at home was my Writer's Workshop. All of my needs as a writer were met, though I never realized it. It was just fun to me—something I enjoyed doing, and something I was proud of. Thinking back, I don't think I even made any connections between writing at home and writing at school. It is best to have Writer's Workshop every day if possible, so students can have many different sessions of sustained writing time throughout the school year. The Writing Process mirrors what book authors do and meets writers' needs. In addition, Writing Workshop and the Writing Process give students the experience and skills they will need to become lifelong writers who find joy in putting their story down on the paper.

References

Avery, C. (2002). . . . *And with a light touch: Learning about reading, writing, and teaching with first graders*. Portsmouth, NH: Heinemann.

Calkins, L., & Ehrenworth, M. (2016). Growing extraordinary writers: Leadership decisions to raise the level of writing across a school and a district. *The Reading Teacher, 70*(1), 7–18.

Cooper, J. D. (2000). *Literacy: Helping children construct meaning*. Boston, MA: Houghton Mifflin Company.

Fletcher, R. (1996). *Breathing in breathing out: Keeping a writer's notebook*. Portsmouth, NH: Heinemann.

Fletcher, R., & Portalupi, J. (2001). *Writing workshop: The essential guide*. Portsmouth, NJ: Heinemann.

Graves, D. (1983). Writing: *Teachers and Children at work*. Exeter, NH: Heinemann.

MacLachlan, P. (1998). *What you know first*. New York: HarperCollins.

Murray, D. (1982). *Learning by teaching*. Montclair, NJ: Boynton/Cook.

Painter, K. (2006). *Living and teaching the writing workshop*. Portsmouth, NH: Heinemann.

Routman, R. (2000). *Conversations: Strategies for teaching, learning, and evaluating*. Portsmouth, NH: Heinemann.

Rylant, C. (1986). *Night in the country*. New York: Simon & Schuster.

Tompkins, G. (2014). *Literacy for the 21st century: A balanced approach*. Boston, MA: Pearson.

CHAPTER 7

Literature for Young Readers

In Ms. Young's third grade class, it is time for Reading Workshop and Ms. Young has just asked students to make sure they had books ready for Drop Everything and Read (DEAR) time. Neika, an African-American girl looks for a book to read. She flips through a couple of books that have animals as main characters, then she spies a book called <u>Hair Love</u> (Cherry & Harrison, 2019) with a picture of a girl who looks just like her on the front. She flips through and sees that it is about a daddy who fixes his daughter's hair. She thinks to herself about how her dad sometimes fixes her hair, too, when her mom has to work. She excitedly scurries off with the book and finds a beanbag chair to lounge in while she reads. She smiles as she turns the pages and thinks about how this little girl is so much like her. When Ms. Young rings the bell to indicate that it is time to end DEAR time, she decides she is ready to make a project about this book. She decides to make a paper bag puppet of the girl from the book, and she plans to do a puppet show to share the book. She uses black yarn for hair, and she colors her puppet's skin with People Colors to look like her skin. She signs up to share her project with the class, then she rereads her book to prepare for the puppet show.

The Importance of Choice

It is important for children to have a choice of what they will read, as we talked about in Chapter 5. If students are able to choose their reading material, they will be much more motivated to read. When they can read something they are interested in, they are much more excited about the reading experience. Just think of how different it is for you when you get to choose a book, as opposed to reading a book that is assigned to you. We would much rather have a choice of what to read.

Many wonderful children's books are available for young readers to choose from. Paterson (1990) identifies simplicity, harmony, and brilliance as the attributes beautiful children's books have in common. Avery (2002) states that "Children are good at recognizing beautiful books. They remember words and phrases" (p. 225). Gallagher (2009) emphasizes the need for students to have interesting books to choose from. He states, "Rather than waiting for students to discover the joys of the library, we must bring the books to the students. Students need to be surrounded by interesting books daily, not just on those occasional days when the teacher takes them to the library" (p. 84). We can help students find just the right book by providing a wide variety of books on different levels that cater to different interests and represent various genres. To entice students to read, it is helpful to provide a reading center where they can easily choose a book, get comfortable, and get lost in the book. Many teachers provide soft chairs, beanbag chairs, pillows, and reading lamps that offer soft lighting to the area. One teacher I know had a reading castle built from wood and painted purple with benches and pillows inside. Her students loved to grab the perfect book and cuddle with a pillow or stuffed animal inside the reading castle.

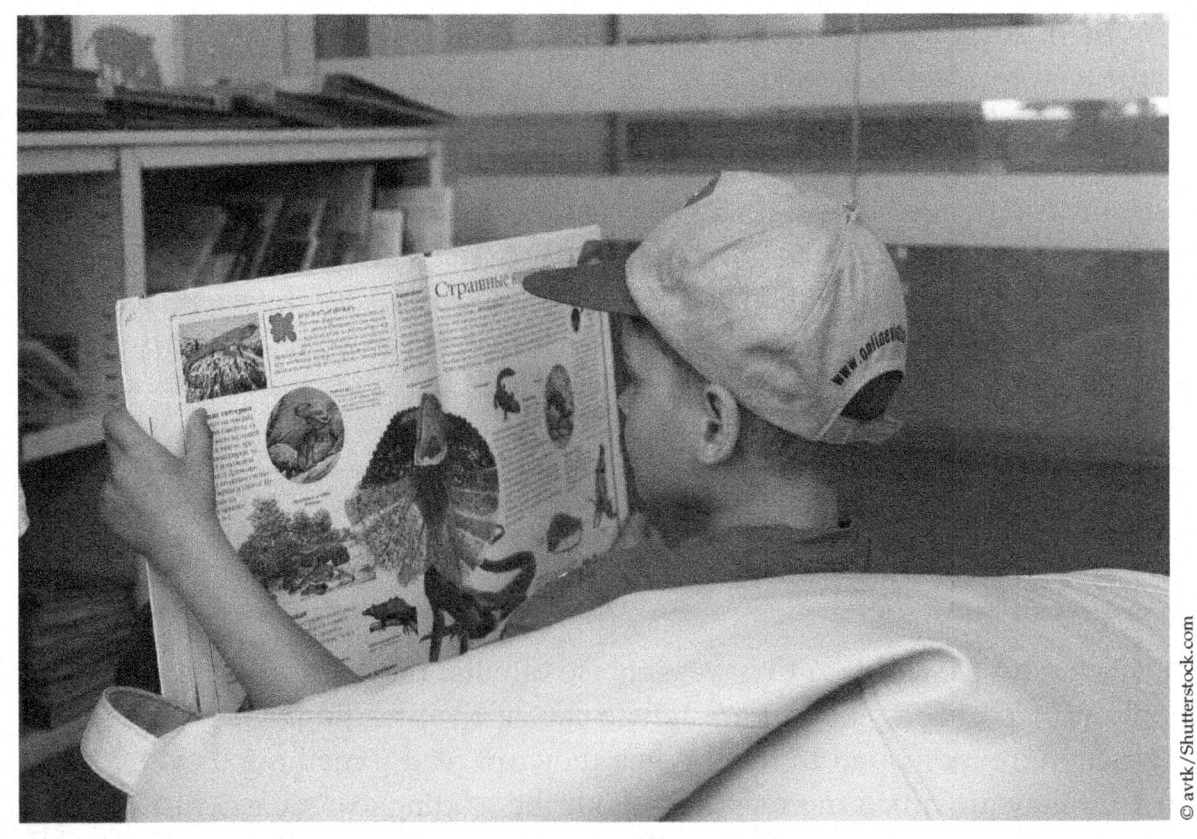

When you are collecting books for your classroom library, there are many different types and genres of books to choose from. Looking for books that will entice young children to read can be really exciting. Avery (2002) recommends looking for books you love, books by favorite authors, well-written books that flow nicely, predictable books, books representing both male and female characters, books whose characters come from many different cultures, books of various topics of interest, and books that go with topics you are teaching. Following are some different types of books to include when you are planning your search.

Predictable Books

Predictable books have patterns and repetition that make the text easier for children to read. Tompkins (2015) states, "Predictable books are often used for shared reading because these books have rhyme, repetition, and patterns that enable young children to read them more easily" (p. 282). The author goes on to say that many predictable books feature familiar songs, questions and answers, numbers, days of the week, and circular stories. The repetition and pattern in predictable books make it easier for children to read along during shared reading (Avery, 2002). According to Templeton and Gehsmann (2014), "These types of books are lots of fun to read with young children and, because they're easily memorized, they can be especially helpful in teaching early reading skills such as alliteration, rhyme awareness, letter recognition, and concept of words in text" (p. 190). Examples of predictable books follow:

Carle, E. (1969). *The very hungry caterpillar.* Cleveland, OH: World Publishing Company.

Carle, E. (1997). *Today is Monday.* New York: Puffin Books.

Fleming, D. (1997). *Barnyard banter.* New York: Henry Holt & Co.

Hill, E. (2003). *Where's Spot?* New York: Puffin Books.

Martin, B., Jr., & Archambault, J. (2009). *Chicka chicka boom boom.* New York: Beach Lane Books.

Calmenson, S. (1996). *Engine, engine, number nine.* New York: Hyperion Books.

Numeroff, L. (1987). *If you give a mouse a cookie.* New York: HarperCollins.

Paparone, P. (2005). *Five little ducks.* New York: Simon & Schuster.

Big Books

Big Books are large copies of a book that can easily be shared with students in a way that they can all see the pictures and the print, and they are often predictable books as well. Children can easily read along as a group in an atmosphere that is nonthreatening, thus encouraging reluctant readers to join in. According to Routman (1988), "we read and sing the poems, Big Books, and stories over and over again. Repeated readings of a book–especially if the book has rhyme, rhythm, and repetition–make it easy for the beginning reader to join in. Fluency and comprehension improve if the students are given continuous practice" (p. 66). Rhodes and Dudley-Marling (1988) suggest that Big Books are perfect for teachers reading to whole groups, because the "large text makes it easy for children to follow along," and that the "novelty of Big Books may also be a special invitation for some children to read" (p. 91). According to Templeton and Gehsmann (2014), Big Books help children learn "how print works–how to begin reading at the top of the page, then read in a left to right motion, and return sweep to the bottom of the page; how books work–the title, the author/illustrator line, the title page, how to turn pages, and. . .the difference between letters and words" (p. 191). Many children's books are available as Big Books. For younger children, it is best to choose Big Books with very few lines on a page. Some of my favorites that I have enjoyed using with students are:

Bridwell, N. (1988). *Clifford's birthday party.* New York: Scholastic, Inc.

Carlson, N. (1990). *I like me!* New York: The Penguin Group.

Cowley, J. (1980). *Mrs. Wishy-Washy.* Los Angeles: Hameray Publishing.

Dillon, L., & Dillon, D. (2002). *Rap a tap tap: Here's Bojangles–think of that!* New York: Blue Sky Press.

Heller, R. (1999). *Chickens aren't the only ones.* New York: Simon & Schuster.

Hoberman, M. (1978). *A house is a house for me.* New York: Viking Press.

Paparone, P. (2005). *Five little ducks.* New York: Simon & Schuster.

Alphabet Books

Many alphabet books are intended to help young readers recognize sounds and learn about letters. This type of book typically has a letter on each page and pictures of things that begin with the letter. Some alphabet books are more complex and include a sentence or short paragraph about the letter or words that begin with the letter. Many alphabet books of this type also include rhyme, alliteration, and rhythm. This type of alphabet book is good for helping students learn vocabulary (Tompkins, 2015) and practice different types of word play. Emergent readers and writers can write their own alphabet books on a topic or theme of choice, using professionally published alphabet books as examples. For instance, if they wanted to write an alphabet book about food, they could write, "*A* is for apple, *B* is for blueberries, *C* is for carrots," and so on. Here are some excellent examples of alphabet books:

Baker, K. (2010). *LMNO peas.* New York: Simon & Schuster.

Bingham, K. (2012). *Z is for moose.* New York: Greenwillow Books.

Ehlert, L. (1989). *Eating the alphabet.* Boston, MA: Houghton Mifflin Harcourt.

Fleming, D. (2002). *Alphabet under construction.* New York: Henry Holt & Co.

Kontis, A. (2006). *AlphaOops: The day Z went first.* Somerville, MA: Candlewick Press.

Lear, E. (2005). *A was once an apple pie.* London: Orchard Books.

Lionni, L. (1968). *The alphabet tree.* New York: Dragonfly Books.

O'Connor, J. (2008). *Fancy Nancy's favorite fancy words: From accessories to zany.* New York: HarperCollins.

Slate, J. (1996). *Miss Bindergarten goes to kindergarten.* New York: Puffin Books.

Van Allsburg, C. (1987). *The Z was zapped.* New York: Houghton Mifflin.

Word Play Books

Word play books include rhyme, alliteration, rhythm, and onomatopoeia, and they help children learn how words work, how they can be similar, how they sound, and how they can represent sounds. Templeton and Gehsmann (2014) state, "...because as a species we may be 'hard-wired' to respond to rhythm and rhyme, sharing poetry, fingerplays, nursery rhymes, and songs with young children and older English learners support their literacy development" (p. 188). In addition, awareness of rhyme is important for phonological and phonemic awareness development. Following are some examples of word play books:

Andreae, G. (1999). *Giraffes can't dance.* New York: Scholastic.

Barretta, G. (2007). *Dear deer: A book of homophones.* New York: Henry Holt & Co.

Cronin, D. (2000). *Click, clack, moo: Cows that type.* New York: Simon & Schuster.

Degan, B. (1985). *Jamberry.* New York: Harper Trophy.

Fox, M. (1988). *Edward the emu.* New York: HarperCollins.

Gibson, A. (2003). *Split! Splat!* New York: Scholastic.

Litwin, E. (2010). *Pete the cat: I love my white shoes.* New York: HarperCollins.

Martin, B., Jr. (1967). *Brown bear, brown bear, what do you see?* New York: Henry Holt & Co.

Moss, L. (1995). *Zin! Zin! Zin! A violin.* New York: Aladdin Paperbacks.

Dr. Seuss (1974). *There's a wocket in my pocket.* Boston, MA: Houghton Mifflin.

Weston, C. (2014). *Ava and Pip.* Naperville, IL: Sourcebooks Jabberwocky.

Wood, A., & Wood, D. (1985). *King Bidgood's in the bathtub.* Orlando, FL: Harcourt Brace & Co.

Concept Books

Concept books are books that teach content, and they can be used in language arts, math, science, or social studies. According to Templeton and Gehsmann (2014), "Concept books help children learn about everyday concepts such as patterns, shapes, colors, numbers, letters, and days of the week" (p. 189), and they can help children develop academic vocabulary associated with the topics. You can find high-quality books that go along with just about any topic you are teaching. Following are some of my favorite concepts books:

Arnold, T. (1997). *Parts.* New York: Penguin Books.

Baer, E. (1990). *This is the way we go to school: A book about children around the world.* New York: Scholastic.

Beaumont, K. (2004). *I like myself!*

Carle, E. (1988). *The mixed-up chameleon.* New York: HarperCollins.

Crews, D. (1968). *Ten black dots.* Hong Kong: South China Printing Company.

Crews, D. (1978). *Freight train.* New York: HarperCollins.

Jeffers, O. (2013). *The day the crayons quit.* New York: Penguin Books.

Hoban, T. (1998). *So many circles, so many squares.* New York: Greenwillow Books.

Lionni, L. (1997). *A color of his own.* New York: Random House.

Dr. Seuss (1968). *The foot book.* New York: Random House.

Wells, R. (1997). *Bunny money.* New York: Penguin Books.

Wordless Picture Books

Wordless picture books "tell a story through illustrations rather than words" (Templeton & Gehsmann, 2014, p. 190). Teachers can use them to help children learn about handling books, how to turn the pages to go from left to right, and how to get meaning from illustrations before they are able to track print. In addition, wordless picture books are excellent to use for children to tell or write stories to go along with the pictures. According to the authors, "Telling stories from pictures alone requires a sophisticated level of inference; for this reason, reading wordless picture books supports children's development of comprehension strategies and thinking skills" (p. 190). Joseph and Annabelle, the two children I tutor, love to talk about illustrations as they read. Joseph's favorite book is *Goodnight, Gorilla* (Rathmann, 2004), a wordless picture book. He points to the pictures and tells the same story every time he reads it. Avery (2002) states, "The reading of wordless picture books is as diverse as the readers who bring meaning to those books" (p. 232). Here are some wordless picture books that are popular:

Briggs, R. (1978). *The snowman.* New York: Random House.

Day, A. (1985). *Good dog, Carl.* New York: Simon & Schuster.

dePaola, T. (1978). *Pancakes for breakfast.* Orlando, FL: Houghton Mifflin Harcourt.

Lehman, B. (2004). *The red book.* New York: Houghton Mifflin Company.

Rathmann, P. (2004). *Goodnight, gorilla.* New York: G. P. Putnam's Sons.

Wiesner, D. (2013). *Mr. Wuffles!* Boston, MA: Houghton Mifflin Harcourt.

Multicultural Books

Every child should see themselves in a book, just like Neika in the scenario. When a child is not able to find a book that has someone who looks like them as a main character, it sends them the message that books are not for them, and reading is not for them. It is important to provide books from all different cultures in the classroom. Especially make sure that you have books that represent the cultures and ethnicities of all students in your class. In addition, teachers should choose books that authentically represent ethnicities and cultures, making sure to avoid stereotypical depictions. Following are some excellent multicultural books to use in the classroom:

Cherry, M., & Harrison, V. (2019). *Hair love.* New York: Penguin Books.

Fox, M. (1997). *Whoever you are.* Orlando, FL: Harcourt.

Katz, K. (2002). *The color of us.* New York: Henry Holt & Co.

Perry, L. (2015). *Hair like mine.* Detroit, MI: G Publishing, LLC.

Perry, L. (2016). *Skin like mine.* Detroit, MI: G Publishing, LLC.

Recorvits, H. (2014). *My name is Yoon.* New York: Frances Foster Books.

Sehgal, S., & Sehgal, K. (2018). *Festival of colors.* New York: Simon & Schuster.

Tarpley, N. A. (2001). *I love my hair.* New York: Little, Brown and Company.

Tonatiuh, D. (2010). *Dear primo: A letter to my cousin.* New York: Abrams Books for Young Readers.

Williams, K. L., & Mohammed, K. (2009). *My name is Sangoel.* Grand Rapids, MI: Eerdmans Books for Young Readers.

Critical Literacy

Templeton states that in the view of critical literacy, ". . .literacy, education, and critical thinking are essential to realize the ideals of liberty, freedom, and social justice" (p. 73). According to Dolan (2012), critical literacy is reading text "in an active and reflective manner which promotes a deeper understanding of socially constructed concepts, such as power, inequality, and injustice in human relationships" (p. 5). Freire and Macedo (1987) told us that human beings "read the word" in order to "read the world," and they emphasized the importance of thinking about the world through a critical lens during experiences with literature. There are many books for children that are perfect for starting critical conversations in the classroom. Books that address ethnicity, gender, the LGBTQ community, culture, language, people with special needs, war, displaced people, and marginalized groups can serve as springboards for critical discussions. Dolan recommends using picture books "for incorporating global and justice perspectives in the classroom" (p. 5). Critical conversations focus on the value of diversity and highlight the power of literacy.

When planning a reading of a critical literacy book, it is a good idea to preview the book and post sticky notes throughout the text where you would like to raise questions to start the conversation. Teachers can introduce new vocabulary through a book introduction or a mini-lesson prior to the reading of the book. During the reading, Meller, Richardson, and Hatch (2009) suggest phrasing questions to "...illicit children's own questions, further their understanding of the issues in the book, and encourage the children to make connections between themselves and the text" (p. 77). After the reading, you can encourage your students to draw a picture or write about the ideas brought up by the text.

It is especially important to include books and critical conversations about issues that are relevant to your classroom setting. For instance, if you have a child in the class who has two mothers, you could read *Heather Has Two Mommies* (Newman, 1989) in order to help your student see that there are other children who have the same kind of family they do. It also helps the other children feel comfortable asking questions and learning about the child's family. Ryan and Hermann-Wilmarth (2018) recommend including LGBTQ literature with young children. They state, "We're convinced that this kind of inclusive teaching can help create more equitable classrooms where LGBTQ students and their families are treated equally and all students are encouraged to learn about the diverse world around them in more nuanced and expansive ways" (p. 1). Here is a list of books that could be used to begin a critical conversation:

Brown, D. (2018). *The truly brave princesses.* China: NubeOcho.

Buitrago, J. (2015). *Two white rabbits.* Berkeley, CA: Groundwood Books.

Bunting, E. (2006). *One green apple.* New York: Clarion Books.

Davids, S. (2015). *Annie's plaid shirt.* Miami, FL: Upswing Press.

dePaola, T. (1979). *Oliver Button is a sissy.* New York: Simon & Schuster.

Herthel, J. (2014). *I am Jazz.* London: The Penguin Books Group.

Isabella, J. (2015). *The red bicycle.* Ontario, Canada: Kids Can Press Ltd.

Lorbiecki, M. (1998). *Sister Anne's hands.* New York: Puffin Books.

Ludwig, T. (2013). *The invisible boy.* New York: Knopf Books for Young Readers.

McKissack, P. (2001). *Goin' someplace special.* New York: Scholastic.

Mora, P. (2000). *Tomas and the library lady.* New York: Dragonfly Books.

Munsch, R. (1999). *The paper bag princess.* Toronto: Annick Press Ltd.

Munson, D. (2000). *Enemy pie.* San Francisco, CA: Chronicle Books.

Newman, L. (1989). *Heather has two mommies.* Somerville, MA: Candlewick Press.

Newman, L. (2009). *Daddy, papa, and me.* Berkeley, CA: Tricycle Press.

Newman, L. (2009). *Mommy, mamma, and me.* Berkeley, CA: Tricycle Press.

Newman, L. (2017). *Sparkle boy.* New York: Lee & Low Books, Inc.

Parnell, P., & Richardson, J. (2005). *And Tango makes three.* New York: Simon & Schuster.

Seskin, S., & Shamblin, A. (2002). *Don't laugh at me.* Berkeley, CA: Tricycle Press.

Smalls, I. (2003). *Don't say ain't.* Watertown, MA: Charlesbridge.

Tonatiuh, D. (2013). *Pancho Rabbit and the Coyote.* New York: Abrams Books for Young Readers.

Tonatiuh, D. (2014). *Separate is never equal.* New York: Scholastic.

Tonatiuh, D. (2018). *Undocumented: A worker's fight.* New York: Abrams ComicArts.

Trottier, M. (2011). *Migrant.* Toronto: Groundwood Books.

Williams, K. L., & Mohammed, K. (2007). *Four feet, two sandals.* Grand Rapids, MI: Eerdmans Books for Young Readers.

Woodson, J. (2001). *The other side.* New York: G. P. Putnam's Sons.

Woodson, J. (2012) *Each kindness.* New York: G. P. Putnam's Sons.

Woodson, J. (2018). *Visiting day.* London: Penguin Books.

As I have talked to both undergraduate and graduate students (who are already teachers), I have asked them how they would use literature about LGBTQ families in the classroom. Many of my students say they understand the need to use literature that represents all students in their classroom, but they are not sure about using books that address the LGBTQ community. They say they are not sure how parents or administrators would react, and they are hesitant to bring up what they see as a controversial topic. What are your thoughts on this dilemma? Would you use LGBTQ book with your students? In what ways would you use them?

Acquiring Books

You can never have too many books in your classroom library, but sometimes you have to get creative when you are trying to stock your shelves. A great place to start is your school library.

Librarians usually love to help you select books for your classroom library, and you can change them out every so often to keep things interesting. Many times, librarians will have books they no longer need that they will give you for your classroom library. You can also ask public libraries if they have any books they are getting rid of, or look at garage sales and thrift shops. Often, when you order books from book clubs, you can get free books with bonus points. Another idea is to suggest to parents that they donate a book to the classroom library in honor of their child's birthday. The main idea is to get as many books of different levels, genres, and topics as you can in order to help your students find that one just right book that will hook them on reading.

Motivating Readers

Students learn to read by reading. The more we can get our students to read, the better readers they will become. Just like anything you want to learn to do, whether it be basketball, knitting, or playing guitar, you must practice to learn how to become proficient. The best way to get students to read is to help them find that perfect book that will hook them on reading, then give them plenty of time to read. Providing many books to choose from is one excellent thing you can do. It is also helpful to find out about children's interests, then seek out books on the topic that match your students' levels that you think they would enjoy.

Another idea to motivate students to read is to send children home with a reading backpack that includes books and a stuffed animal. Students can take turns taking the backpacks home, and you can encourage them to read to their stuffed animals and to their family. In my classroom, I called the bags "Snuggle Up and Read Bags." I had five bags, each with different books and different stuffed animals. I rotated the bags among the students to take home over the weekend. I changed up the books, once all students had taken them home. The children loved the bags, and they were so excited when it was their turn to take them home. There are many different variations of these book bags. Sometimes, teachers will send home books in a bag, and the student reads the book with their family, then writes or makes something in response to the book to bring back and share with the class.

Book talks can also motivate students to read. You can do a quick book talk each morning, giving enough information to entice the students to read the book, then place the book in the book center. It is also fun for the students to do book talks to encourage their classmates to read a book they have enjoyed. Atwell (2007) describes student book talks as short talks telling about a book they love. She doesn't encourage props or even notes about what her students want to say. Book talks are organic messages about something they enjoyed reading and would like to recommend to their friends. You can also ask parents to come in and do book talks of favorite books.

Another example of a fun and motivating activity is to read *Flat Stanley* (Brown, 1964), then to have all students make a Flat Stanley out of manila paper, then laminate it. Students can take Flat Stanley home, take pictures of him at home or wherever they go, then write about Flat Stanley's adventures. I had a Flat Stanley that I took everywhere with me and took pictures. I would come back to school, show the pictures to the kids, then tell the students stories about what Flat Stanley did. My sister-in-law even took him to England with her and took pictures. The students were so excited to see the pictures when Flat Stanley got back from England! Another variation is for students to make a flat version of themselves to take home, then write about the adventures of their "flat self."

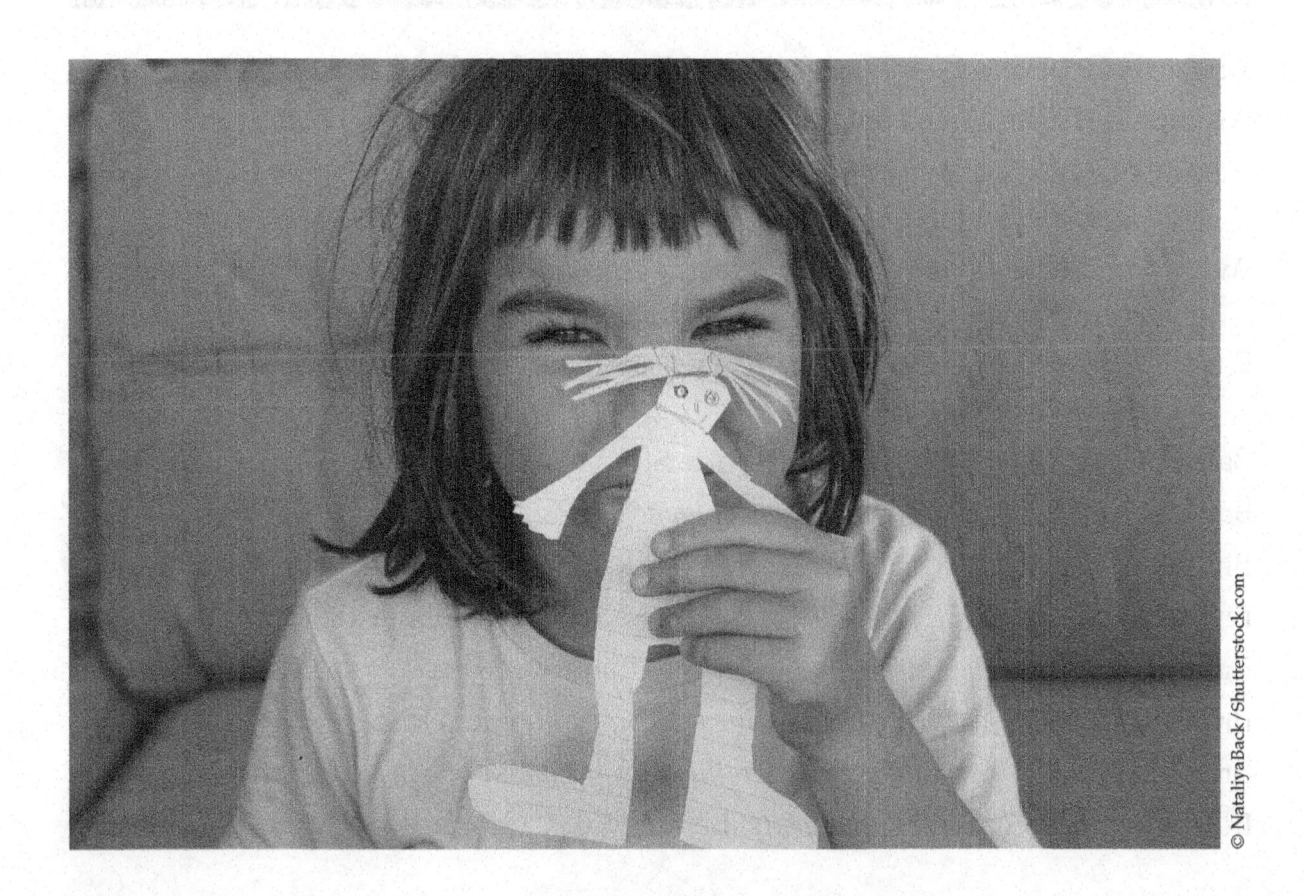

One school where I taught had an Everybody Reads Day each year. The day was filled with reading activities. We went outside to read on blankets under a tree, we had guest readers from the community, we had a visit from Clifford the Big Red Dog (a costumed teacher—actually me!), and students dressed up as their favorite book characters. Each grade level had a different art activity they did to represent books they had read. Some made book characters out of soda bottles, and others made them from paper bags. Still others did cereal box book reports or mobiles representing the characters, setting, and plot of a book. We lined the halls of our school with the characters and projects, then had a book character parade through the school.

It is important to provide just the right book in order to hook every child in our class on reading. We must do everything we can to motivate our students to read, and we must give them sustained times every day to read. Gallagher (2009) implores us to "never lose sight that our highest priority is to raise students who become lifelong readers. What our students read in school is important; what they read the rest of their lives is more important" (p. 117).

References

Andreae, G. (1999). *Giraffes can't dance.* New York: Scholastic.

Arnold, T. (1997). *Parts.* New York: Penguin Books.

Atwell, N. (2007). The reading zone: How to help kids become skilled, passionate, habitual, critical readers. New York: Scholastic.

Avery, C. (2002). *. . . And with a light touch: Learning about reading, writing, and teaching with first graders.* Portsmouth, NH: Heinemann.

Baer, E. (1990). *This is the way we go to school: A book about children around the world.* New York: Scholastic.

Baker, K. (2010). *LMNO peas.* New York: Simon & Schuster.

Barretta, G. (2007). *Dear deer: A book of homophones.* New York: Henry Holt & Co.

Bingham, K. (2012). *Z is for moose.* New York: Greenwillow Books.

Bridwell, N. (1988). *Clifford's birthday party.* New York: Scholastic, Inc.

Briggs, R. (1978). *The snowman.* New York: Random House.

Brown, D. (2018). *The truly brave princesses.* China: NubeOcho.

Brown, J. (1964). *Flat Stanley: His original adventure.* New York: HarperCollins.

Buitrago, J. (2015). *Two white rabbits.* Berkeley, CA: Groundwood Books.

Bunting, E. (2006). *One green apple.* New York: Clarion Books.

Carle, E. (1969). *The very hungry caterpillar.* Cleveland, OH: World Publishing Company.

Carle, E. (1988). *The mixed-up chameleon.* New York: HarperCollins.

Carle, E. (1997). *Today is Monday.* New York: Puffin Books.

Carlson, N. (1990). *I like me!* New York: Puffin Books.

Cherry, M., & Harrison, V. (2019). *Hair love.* New York: Penguin Books.

Cowley, J. (1980). *Mrs. Wishy-Washy.* Los Angeles: Hameray Publishing.

Crews, D. (1968). *Ten black dots.* Hong Kong: South China Printing Company.

Crews, D. (1978). *Freight train.* New York: HarperCollins.

Cronin, D. (2000). *Click, clack, moo: Cows that type.* New York: Simon & Schuster.

Davids, S. (2015). *Annie's plaid shirt.* Miami, FL: Upswing Press.

Day, A. (1985). *Good dog, Carl.* New York: Simon & Schuster.

Jeffers, O. (2013). *The day the crayons quit.* New York: Penguin Books.

Degan, B. (1985). *Jamberry.* New York: Harper Trophy.

dePaola, T. (1978). *Pancakes for breakfast.* Orlando, FL: Houghton Mifflin Harcourt.

dePaola, T. (1979). *Oliver Button is a sissy.* New York: Simon & Schuster.

Dillon, L., & Dillon, D. (2002). *Rap a tap tap: Here's Bojangles–think of that!* New York: Blue Sky Press.

Dolan, A (2012) 'The Potential of Picture Books for Teaching Migration as a Geographical Theme'. 33rd IBBY International Congress: Crossing Boundaries: Translations and Migrations 23rd-26th August 2012, Imperial College, London.

Ehlert, L. (1989). *Eating the alphabet.* Boston, MA: Houghton Mifflin Harcourt.

Fox, M. (1988). *Edward the emu.* New York: HarperCollins.

Fox, M. (1997). *Whoever you are.* Orlando, FL: Harcourt.

Fleming, D. (1997). *Barnyard banter.* New York: Henry Holt & Co.

Fleming, D. (2002). *Alphabet under construction.* New York: Henry Holt & Co.

Freire, P., & Macedo, D. (1987). *Literacy: Reading the word and the world.* Boulder, CO: Routledge.

Gallagher, K. (2009). *Readicide: How schools are killing reading and what we can do about it.* Portland, ME: Stenhouse Publishers.

Gibson, A. (2003). *Split! Splat!* New York: Scholastic.

Heller, R. (1999). *Chickens aren't the only ones.* New York: Simon & Schuster.

Herthel, J. (2014). *I am Jazz.* London: The Penguin Books Group.

Hill, E. (2003). *Where's Spot?* New York: Puffin Books.

Hoban, T. (1998). *So many circles, so many squares.* New York: Greenwillow Books.

Hoberman, M. (1978). *A house is a house for me.* New York: Viking Press.

Isabella, J. (2015). *The red bicycle.* Ontario, Canada: Kids Can Press Ltd.

Katz, K. (2002). *The color of us.* New York: Henry Holt & Co.

Kontis, A. (2006). *AlphaOops: The day Z went first.* Somerville, MA: Candlewick Press.

Lear, E. (2005). *A was once an apple pie.* London: Orchard Books.

Lehman, B. (2004). *The red book.* New York: Houghton Mifflin Company.

Lionni, L. (1968). *The alphabet tree.* New York: Dragonfly Books.

Lionni, L. (1997). *A color of his own.* New York: Random House.

Litwin, E. (2010). *Pete the cat: I love my white shoes.* New York: HarperCollins.

Lorbiecki, M. (1998). *Sister Anne's hands.* New York: Puffin Books.

Ludwig, T. (2013). *The invisible boy.* New York: Knopf Books for Young Readers.

Martin, B., Jr. (1967). *Brown bear, brown bear, what do you see?* New York: Henry Holt & Co.

Martin, B., Jr., & Archambault, J. (2009). *Chicka chicka boom boom.* New York: Beach Lane Books.

McKissack, P. (2001). *Goin' someplace special.* New York: Scholastic.

Calmenson, S. (1996). *Engine, engine, number nine.* New York: Hyperion Books.

Meller, W., Richardson, D., & Hatch, J. (2009). Using read-alouds with critical literacy literature in K-3 classrooms. *Young Children, 64* (6).

Mora, P. (2000). *Tomas and the library lady.* New York: Dragonfly Books.

Moss, L. (1995). *Zin! Zin! Zin! A violin.* New York: Aladdin Paperbacks.

Munsch, R. (1999). *The paper bag princess.* Toronto: Annick Press Ltd.

Munson, D. (2000). *Enemy pie.* San Francisco, CA: Chronicle Books.

Newman, L. (1989). *Heather has two mommies.* Somerville, MA: Candlewick Press.

Newman, L. (2009). *Daddy, papa, and me.* Berkley, CA: Tricycle Press.

Newman, L. (2009). *Mommy, mamma, and me.* Berkeley, CA: Tricycle Press.

Newman, L. (2017). *Sparkle boy.* New York: Lee & Low Books, Inc.

Numeroff, L. (1987). *If you give a mouse a cookie.* New York: HarperCollins.

O'Connor, J. (2008). *Fancy Nancy's favorite fancy words: From accessories to zany.* New York: HarperCollins.

Paparone, P. (2005). *Five little ducks.* New York: Simon & Schuster.

Parnell, P., & Richardson, J. (2005). *And Tango makes three.* New York: Simon & Schuster.

Paterson, K. (1990). Heart in hiding. In W. Zinsser (Ed.), *Worlds of childhood: The art and craft of writing for children.* Boston, MA: Houghton Mifflin.

Perry, L. (2015). *Hair like mine.* Detroit, MI: G Publishing, LLC.

Perry, L. (2016). *Skin like mine.* Detroit, MI: G Publishing, LLC.

Rathmann, P. (2004). *Goodnight, gorilla.* New York: G. P. Putnam's Sons.

Recorvits, H. (2014). *My name is Yoon.* New York: Frances Foster Books.

Rhodes, L., & Dudley-Marling, C. (1988). *Readers and writers with a difference: A holistic approach to teaching learning disabled and remedial students.* Portsmouth, NH: Heinemann.

Routman, R. (1988). *Transitions: From literature to literacy.* Portsmouth, NH: Heinemann.

Ryan, C., & Hermann-Wilmarth, J. (2018). *Reading the rainbow: LGBTQ-inclusive literacy instruction in the elementary classroom.* New York: Teachers College Press.

Sehgal, S., & Sehgal, K. (2018). *Festival of colors.* New York: Simon & Schuster.

Seskin, S., & Shamblin, A. (2002). *Don't laugh at me.* Berkeley, CA: Tricycle Press.

Dr. Seuss (1968). *The foot book.* New York: Random House.

Dr. Seuss (1974). *There's a wocket in my pocket.* Boston, MA: Houghton Mifflin.

Slate, J. (1996). *Miss Bindergarten goes to kindergarten.* New York: Puffin Books.

Smalls, I. (2003). *Don't say ain't.* Watertown, MA: Charlesbridge.

Tarpley, N. A. (2001). *I love my hair.* New York: Little, Brown and Company.

Templeton, S., & Gehsmann, K. (2014). *Teaching reading and writing: The developmental approach.* Boston, MA, Pearson.

Tompkins, G. (2015). *Literacy in the early grades: A successful start for PreK-4 readers and writers.* Boston, MA: Pearson.

Tonatiuh, D. (2010). *Dear primo: A letter to my cousin.* New York: Abrams Books for Young Readers.

Tonatiuh, D. (2013). *Pancho Rabbit and the Coyote.* New York: Abrams Books for Young Readers.

Tonatiuh, D. (2014). *Separate is never equal.* New York: Scholastic.

Tonatiuh, D. (2018). *Undocumented: A worker's fight.* New York: Abrams ComicArts.

Trottier, M. (2011). *Migrant.* Toronto: Groundwood Books.

Van Allsburg, C. (1987). *The Z was zapped.* New York: Houghton Mifflin.

Wells, R. (1997). *Bunny money.* New York: Penguin Books.

Weston, C. (2014). *Ava and Pip.* Naperville, IL: Sourcebooks Jabberwocky.

Wiesner, D. (2013). *Mr. Wuffles!* Boston, MA: Houghton Mifflin Harcourt.

Williams, K. L., & Mohammed, K. (2007). *Four feet, two sandals.* Grand Rapids, MI: Eerdmans Books for Young Readers.

Williams, K. L., & Mohammed, K. (2009). *My name is Sangoel.* Grand Rapids, MI: Eerdmans Books for Young Readers.

Wood, A., & Wood, D. (1985). *King Bidgood's in the bathtub.* Orlando, FL: Harcourt Brace & Co.

Woodson, J. (2001). *The other side.* New York: G. P. Putnam's Sons.

Woodson, J. (2012). *Each kindness.* New York: G. P. Putnam's Sons.

Woodson, J. (2018). *Visiting day.* London: Penguin Books.

CHAPTER 8

The Multicultural Classroom

Mr. Williams has asked his Kindergarteners to create a self-portrait of themselves, using People Colors crayons to match their skin color. He places a mirror on each table, and the children excitedly look into the mirror and choose crayons and hold them up to their skin to find just the right shade. There is a busy hum in the classroom as children trade crayons and make suggestions of colors their friends can use. After everyone is finished with their pictures, Mr. Williams has each child share their portrait, and they talk together about how each one is different and each one is beautiful. Then he posts them on the walls of the classroom. Next, Mr. Williams asks the students to come to the carpet for story time. He says, "Boys and girls, as you know, we have books in our classroom about all kinds of children—Black children, Hispanic children, White children, Asian children, and Native American children. Today, we have a book about a little Black girl and her daddy. Her daddy helps her fix her hair, and at first he has a lot of trouble, but then he does a really good job!" The children smile and giggle as they imagine their daddy fixing their hair, then they listen intently as Mr. Williams reads Hair Love (Cherry, 2019). Afterward, he shows them the short film, "Hair Love." After the film, Mr. Williams and the class discuss what they like about the book and the film. Jenny says that her daddy fixes her hair, and other children share that their mom helps them fix their hair. Marcus says that his grandmother is in a wheelchair, just like the little girl's mom in the book. Mr. Williams then asks the children to go back to their seats and write or draw something about the book and the film. The children scurry to their workspaces, chattering about what they are going to write and draw.

Including all Cultures

It is important for all students to feel that they are valued in the classroom. Teachers should ensure that all students' cultures are represented in the classroom through literature, images, and activities. Multiculturalism should be a thread that runs throughout your curriculum and should be part of every day. In *White Teacher*, Paley (1979) reflects on being a Jewish child in a Gentile school and feeling that her teachers denied her Jewishness by not acknowledging it. Paley relates her experience to the experiences of minority students, whose white teachers say, "There is no color difference in my classroom. All my children look alike to me." She quotes an African-American mother as saying, "My children are black. They don't look like your children. They know they're black, and we want it recognized. It's a positive difference, an interesting difference, and a comfortable difference" (p. 12). Celebrating multiculturalism in your classroom helps students realize the beauty in the differences we all bring to the classroom.

Banks and Banks (1993) suggest that teachers should examine five areas or dimensions of multicultural education in order to acknowledge issues involved in multicultural education and make learning relevant for children of all cultures.

These five dimensions include content integration, the knowledge construction process, prejudice reduction, an empowering school culture, and an equity pedagogy.

Content integration "deals with the extent to which teachers use examples and content from a variety of cultures and groups to illustrate key concepts, principles, generalizations, and theories in their subject area or discipline," according to Banks and Banks (1993, p. 21). Banks and Banks state that these integrations must be logical rather than contrived. He goes on to state, however, that although some content areas more than others lend themselves to content integration, all content area teachers should attempt to integrate different cultures into their lessons.

Derman-Sparks (1989) suggests some methods for integrating multicultural or antibias content into the day of an early childhood classroom. According to Derman-Sparks, a teacher can provide art materials that are representative of all skin colors, such as brown and black construction paper, tempera paint, and clay. As illustrated in the scenario, crayons and markers are available in a variety of skin colors. The teacher can frequently refer to the children's skin color with statements such as, "You are using a beautiful chocolate brown–it matches your skin (hair, eyes)" (p. 25). One year, my first grade students were using the People Colors crayons, and the kids began to hold the crayons up to each other to see which color matched them the best. They were very serious about choosing the right color to represent their skin color, and they were concerned that there wasn't one that matched their skin perfectly.

In the dramatic play center, an early childhood teacher can provide props for portraying a variety of jobs, including both blue-collar and white-collar jobs. The teacher can also provide cooking tools from various ethnic groups and encourage both boys and girls to play together in the home center in nonstereotypical roles. Derman-Sparks (1989) also suggests hanging pictures or posters showing families from a wide variety of ethnic groups, families with different types of organization, and families that have differently abled members. It is important to remember that some families have two moms or dads, some families have single parents or children being raised by grandparents, and other families are blended. Another suggestion is to provide full-length mirrors and engage children in conversations about their skin, hair, and eye color.

Derman-Sparks (1989) states that all puzzles should show diversity, but not stereotypes of ethnic groups. Blocks and other manipulatives should include the colors brown and black. Small people figures used for riding in trucks should include all skin colors, as well as both men and women. Teachers should encourage all students, including girls and differently abled students to participate in activities involving large motor equipment, blocks, and trucks.

According to Derman-Sparks (1989), dolls of all ethnic groups should be available in the early childhood classroom. If children are reluctant to play with a doll different from themselves, the teacher can invite them to play and hold, feed, or take care of the racially different doll—to babysit—so that they can become more comfortable with the different-looking doll. Derman-Sparks also recommends having the children experiment with water to wash the dolls and then engaging them in conversations about how the skin color does not wash off of the dolls—just like skin color does not wash off of people.

For group time, Derman-Sparks (1989) suggests talking about different skin colors, comparing hands, comparing faces in the mirror, feeling and discussing the texture of other people's hair, and comparing photographs of everyone's families. She also describes how the teacher can write a personalized book about each child, describing their physical features, what they like to do, and the child's gender. The teacher can read a different personalized book every day during group time. In addition, the teacher should read many commercially made books depicting people of different races and ethnic groups and engage children in conversations about them. Also during group time, the children can sing songs in different languages and use sign language. In the early childhood classroom that Derman-Sparks describes, multicultural awareness is stressed in all learning areas and is a part of everyday life.

Hale (1982) also gives an example of the way a holiday might be studied in the early childhood classroom. Instead of studying Thanksgiving from the Pilgrim's perspective, they would discuss the oppression experienced by the Native Americans. Similarly, Derman-Sparks (1989) recommends telling the story of "Christopher Columbus's mistake" and studying Native Americans in an authentic way, showing pictures of contemporary Native Americans and their homes, and discussing different aspects of their cultures (p. 89). She also points out that it is important to recognize specific Native American groups, such as Hopi, Navajo, and Cherokee, rather than imply that Native Americans are all the same.

According to Banks and Banks (1993), "The knowledge construction process relates to the extent to which teachers help students to understand, investigate, and determine how the implicit cultural assumptions, frames of references, perspectives, and biases within a discipline influence the ways in which knowledge is constructed within it" (p. 21). Banks and Banks give the examples of scientific racism, and how students can study about it in science class; and the European discovery of America, which can be investigated in Social Studies class.

According to Hale (1982), the white culture is the culture of the school and is thought, by most, to be the norm—the American culture. American education has served the function of preparing children of all cultures to value and accept white culture. The author states, "It is generally assumed that the physical development of all children conforms to the pattern identified for white children" (p. 169). She notes that typically, African-American children are allowed complete freedom of movement at home and adds that many African-American children are seen as being behavior problems because they don't conform to the white standards of behavior.

Kuykendall (1992) states that schools have been found guilty of "class bias and elitism" (p. 34) by only teaching part of history and literature, leaving out contributions from Black, Hispanic, and other cultures. History has been depicted in the manner in which the white culture has constructed it. According to Kuykendall, "when youth were denied their history, they were unlikely to realize their full potential" (p. 34).

Banks and Banks (1993) also describe prejudice reduction as "lessons and activities teachers use to help students develop positive attitudes toward different racial, ethnic, and cultural groups" (p. 22). He suggests that using positive images and examples of people from a variety of cultures will help the students to develop a more positive attitude toward people of different cultures.

Derman-Sparks (1989) recommends the following steps for dealing with children in an early childhood classroom who are responding to cultural differences negatively: "(1) immediately address a child's negative response to a cultural difference, (2) help the child figure out why he or she is uncomfortable, (and) (3) explain what responses are hurtful and offer alternate responses" (p. 70). For example, when a young white girl heard the name of a Japanese visitor, she said "yuck, yuck, yucky." The visitor responded by asking, "Does my name sound funny to you? Have you ever heard it before? It is a new and different name to you. I like my name. It is a Japanese name" (p. 69). The children must learn that it is not OK to say hurtful things about another person's culture.

For dealing with exclusion behaviors, Derman-Sparks (1989) suggests: "set limits, intervene immediately, comfort the target of the discriminatory behavior, and determine the real reasons for the conflict" (p. 71). If you suspect that prejudice does "underlie the exclusion" (p. 71), the child must be told that it is not OK to exclude someone because of their skin color, gender, or culture. The teacher may have to speak to the parents and work up a plan to stop the exclusion behavior. Derman-Sparks warns teachers not to ignore the behavior or excuse it. If discriminatory behavior is going to be stopped, it must be addressed every time.

Derman-Sparks (1989) suggests several activities and experiences that will challenge children's stereotypic ideas. She recommends inviting people to talk to the class that have nonstereotypic jobs for their gender, such as a male nurse, a female doctor, a female firefighter, etc. She also suggests "comparing authentic and stereotypic images in books and other materials" (p. 74) making a class book showing "fair and unfair" (p. 74) pictures, and critiquing books that have stereotypic material in them. Additionally, Derman-Sparks suggests praising children for showing an awareness of stereotypes, discrimination, and prejudice. For example, when a little boy commented that all of the Lego people were white, his teacher responded by saying, "Hey, you're right. There should be Black and Asian and Hispanic figures too...I'm proud of you for noticing because it is important to notice when things are unfair like that" (p. 75).

Derman-Sparks also recommends reading children's books that address prejudice, such as *The Swimming Hole* (Beim & Beim, 1947), *The Sneetches* (Seuss, 1961), and *A Look at Prejudice and Understanding* (Anders, 1976). She goes on to suggest using "persona dolls," dolls made with different skin colors or dolls with disabilities to tell stories about incidents that include examples of prejudice or discriminatory behavior (1989, p. 16). The children can problem solve and come up with suggestions to remedy the problem. Derman-Sparks further advises to "help children learn how to help each other when a discriminatory incident occurs in their classroom" (p. 76), and "to help children learn to take action against bias" (p. 76).

Banks and Banks (1993) refer to Allport's "content hypothesis" that the following conditions must be present in order to improve the students' relations with and attitudes toward different ethnic groups: "equal status, cooperation rather than competition, sanction by authorities such as teachers and administrators; and . . . interpersonal interactions in which students become acquainted as individuals" (p. 22).

Another dimension of multicultural education that Banks and Banks (1993) describe is an empowering school culture, in which everyone in the school buys into a multicultural philosophy and commits themselves to restructuring the school so as to promote gender, racial, and social-class equity.

According to Derman-Sparks (1989), in order to restructure an early childhood classroom to promote antibias curriculum, a teacher needs to make a personal commitment and add multicultural content a little at a time and to make it a priority. It is also helpful to have a support group of other teachers who are implementing the same kinds of things. "We need the diverse perspectives and honest feedback of peers to develop the insights for rethinking how we teach" (p. 112). Derman-Sparks also comments that "it is not necessary to know all the answers before you get started in the classroom" (p. 112). Nobody knows all the answers, she states. Teachers learn more about antibias curriculum as they go along, trying new things, and reflecting on successes as well as failures. The author suggests consciousness-raising activities to explore one's own feelings and attitudes toward multiculturalism. The author recommends going slowly, adding one thing at a time and discussing the results with the support group. She states, "Anti-bias is not a subject you can teach and be done with; it's a way of life . . . you teach anti-bias by living it" (p. 118).

Equity pedagogy is, according to Banks and Banks (1993), analysis on the part of teachers of "teaching procedures and styles to determine the extent to which they reflect multicultural issues and concerns" (p. 22). According to Gay (In Banks & Banks, 1993), most teachers "enter the profession assuming that all students can be taught as if they were European Americans" (p. 213), and "most teachers know little about different ethnic groups' life-styles or learning habits and preferences" (p. 213). Banks and Banks state that "an equity pedagogy exists when teachers modify their teaching in ways that will facilitate the academic achievement of students from diverse racial, cultural, gender, and social-class groups" (p. 22). Teachers can do book studies on books such as *Transforming Teacher Education for Social Justice* (Zygmunt & Clark, 2016) to help them think and plan how they will create a school environment that encourages equity pedagogy and promotes multiculturalism.

English Learners

Any student who speaks a language other than English and is learning English is considered to be an English learner (EL). ELs face many challenges that mainstream students do not. They may feel isolated, shy, and embarrassed, and they may feel that they are not part of the group. In addition, they are learning to read and write, just as other students are, but they are having to learn a whole new language at the same time. Teachers can make things easier for ELs, especially those who are newcomers, by preparing for them and planning ahead of time. Claire and Haynes (1994) state, "what happens the first day will impact your newcomer's confidence, motivation, social adjustment, desire to learn, and even health and attendance" (p. 8). Berg and Miller (2011) suggest preparing the class to welcome newcomers into the community of learners by talking about what it might be like to come to a new place where they do not know anyone. Teachers can use books such as *I Hate English* (Levine, 1989), *Where is Taro* (Claire, 1994), and *Crow Boy* (Yashima, 1955) to encourage a discussion about what it is like to come to a new place where you don't speak the language (Berg & Miller, 2011). The authors recommend assigning a buddy to the newcomer to help them learn about classroom norms and to be their guide. It is even better if you can find a child who speaks the same language as the newcomer to be their buddy. Berg and Miller also emphasize the importance of finding out as much background information as possible about the student and learning about their culture and where they came from.

It is also important to do a variety of assessments to determine the child's English language proficiency, knowledge of letters and sight words, and concepts about print in both languages. Finding out what the child knows and can do and where the child is in terms of literacy, can help you design instruction that will cater to the child's individual needs (Berg & Miller, 2011). Cooper and Kiger (2008) emphasize how important it is for ELs to be in a print-rich environment. The authors state that the EL should be immersed in the action of classroom, and the teacher should be "bubbling with speech" (p. 261). "It doesn't matter that the child doesn't understand all the words," they state, "What matters is that the child feels a part of the class" (p. 261). Cooper and Kiger state, "ELL children need to be steeped in the English language" (p. 261).

Sheltered instruction provides ELs with an environment that supports students as they are learning English. Seidlitz (2019) describes "sheltered English" as "language that is surrounded by enough context clues for language learners with sufficient background to be able to understand what is being communicated" (p. 7). Templeton and Gehsmann (2014) emphasize the importance of building ELs background knowledge so they will have the information they need to understand the content. According to Seidlitz, the main goals of sheltered instruction are "to make content comprehensible to English learners" and "to develop academic language" (p. 7). Through sheltered instruction, teachers provide ELs with scaffolding, visuals, gestures, sentence stems, and plenty of time to talk throughout the day and practice their new language. It is important that ELs are able to read, write, listen, and speak English in every lesson every day in order to become proficient in English.

According to Seidlitz (2019), "In the context of language development, scaffolding provides specific targeted support so that students gradually become self-sufficient in their language production" (p. 40). The author identifies oral, procedural, and instructional scaffolding (as discussed in Chapter 1) as being important for the language development of ELs. Teachers can scaffold a lesson by giving a mini-lesson with visuals and graphic organizers, then having students discuss in their groups what was talked about. Next students could read a short paragraph or passage about the topic, while taking notes. Students could then get into groups, and the teacher could give students sentence stems to complete on chart paper about the content. Students could then go on a gallery walk to view other groups' charts and take notes on an index card about the charts. Finally, students could be asked to do a quick write on a question or statement involving the topic, using their notes. Afterward, students can share what they wrote with their shoulder partner. In this lesson, students would use reading, writing, speaking, and listening while interacting with the content in several different ways.

Seidlitz (2019) states, "Incorporating visuals in our lessons dramatically increases student ability to understand class lessons and discussions" (p. 63). Visuals can be pictures, videos, charts, virtual reality glasses, concrete objects, and graphic organizers. Using visuals gives students "access to content in spite of possible barriers such as lack of background on the subject or limited English proficiency," (p. 63) according to Seidlitz.

Gestures can be as simple as pointing to various words, pictures, or objects throughout the room. For example, a teacher could point to her mouth to encourage students to look at and listen to her, or she could point to an object and say the name of the object and motion to the students to repeat. Gestures can also be used to reinforce specific content. For instance, teachers can make up motions to go with something students are learning. One example might be remembering the parts of a story by raising both hands for "setting," clapping hands for "characters," and putting hands on hips for "plot." Students will associate the movement with the words and remember them more easily.

Sentence stems, or sentences starters, provide students with the first part of a sentence and a blank for the student to complete, which enables them to respond to a question or phrase to form a complete sentence. "Using sentence stems dramatically changes the quality and tone of a classroom because it helps students become increasingly more comfortable using academic language for expression," states Seidlitz (p. 47). The author suggests that students use sentence stems in a small group to take turns completing the sentence. Not only does this give ELs access to the language they will need to form their answer, but it gives them the opportunity to listen to each of their peers as they complete the same stem. When called on to share out to the whole group, the student has had time to formulate and rehearse a response. Speaking in complete sentences also helps students improve both oral and written communication. Seidlitz reminds us, "Teachers must remember that students have trouble writing in ways they cannot speak" (p. 45).

One activity Seidlitz (2019) recommends to incorporate sentence stems is a type of structured conversation called Question, Signal, Stem, Share, Assess (QSSSA). In QSSSA, the teacher asks a question to help students think about a topic, and when they know how they will answer the question, they show a signal, such as a thumbs-up or standing behind their chair. The signal shows the teacher when students are ready, and it gives built-in wait time to ensure everyone has adequate time to think.

Next, the teacher gives students a sentence stem based upon the question. For the share part of the activity, students take turns completing the sentence stem orally in their group. They know that one person from each group will share out to the whole group, and each student gets to practice what they will say if they are called on. In the assess step, the teacher randomly calls on someone to share from each group or has everyone write down their response. Here is an example of a QSSSA lesson:

Q: Why do you think the hungry caterpillar ate so much food?

S: Stand behind your chair when you can answer the question.

S: I think the hungry caterpillar ate so much food because _____.

S: Numbered heads: students number off and everyone shares their stem.

A: Stand up if you are number three to share your stem.

One variation is for groups to come up with a group response after everyone has shared. Group members make sure everyone knows the group response and will be prepared to share. Seidlitz states, "Teachers who facilitate a learning environment using structured conversations provide consistent and systematic oral language practice and support for ELs" (p. 69).

One of the most important things to remember about ELs is that they need to have the opportunity to read, write, listen, and speak all day every day (Seidlitz & Perryman, 2011). Motley (2016) stresses that students, rather than the teacher should be doing the majority of the talk in the classroom. The author recommends that students read, write, and talk and listen to their peers about the content throughout the day in order to form an understanding and internalize the content. According to Seidlitz (2019), teachers must be purposeful in their teaching in order to make the learning understandable to ELs. The author recommends teachers ensure total participation, which "requires the inclusion of all students in the classroom regardless of their language level or ability" (p. 29). Total participation can occur when you do activities such as QSSSA, which requires a response from all students, rather than one or two students answering questions in a whole group setting. According to Seidlitz and Perryman (2011), total participation ensures "every student, during every activity, is involved in listening, writing, speaking, or reading" (p. 98). ELs learn English by using English throughout the day in authentic, meaningful literacy activities with support from the teacher. Remember to always include plans for ELs as you are making plans. Consideration for ELs should not be an add-on or incidental, but it should be at the heart of your lesson planning.

Accepting Home Languages

According to Tompkins (2014), the English spoken in schools is formal English, or what is sometimes referred to as "Standard English." Many children come from communities in which a dialect other than formal English is spoken. These dialects are not inferior to formal English, but they are simply different. Because formal English is used in schools, colleges, and many career settings, teachers must teach students to communicate using formal English. Tompkins states that rather than replace students' home language with formal English, the idea is for students to learn to use a variety of registers and to know when to use each one. Freire and Macedo (1987) state that teachers must "develop radical pedagogical structures that provide students with the opportunity to use their own reality as a basis of literacy. This includes, obviously, the language they bring to the classroom. To do otherwise is to deny students the rights that lie at the core of the notion of an emancipatory literacy" (p. 151). Goodman (1965, 1973) has emphasized the need for acceptance of dialects that differ from school English in the classroom, and that children need to become fluent readers in their own dialect before they can begin to learn school English. Goodman further states that a teacher should attend to a child's meaning instead of making corrections for dialect. Derman-Sparks (1989), Paley (1979, 1995), and Hale (1982) discuss the need for making learning relevant for all cultures represented in the classroom, rather than teaching to the dominant culture. They stress that each culture should be recognized, celebrated, and valued. The language and dialects spoken by all students should also be accepted.

The educational system in the United States today is designed in such a way that the white, middle-class culture will be perpetuated. Middle-class children, in particular, white, middle-class children come to school equipped with the tools necessary to participate in the school culture, because they are already a part of the dominant culture (Delpit, 1988). Delpit concludes that members of a culture transmit cultural rules and codes to comembers implicitly. She states that "when implicit codes are attempted across cultures, communication frequently breaks down" (p. 123). Children of the white, middle-class culture already have what they need to communicate through oral and printed word in ways that ensure their success in the mainstream culture of the school. Because minority children do not belong to the mainstream culture, Delpit points out that they need to be explicitly taught the rules and conventions of the mainstream culture in order to succeed in school. The hidden rules of the dominant culture include the rules of school English, or formal English. Children's home language should be accepted and respected by the school while the child is learning the rules of school English.

Miller and Higgins (2006) state, "Both public figures and educational experts acknowledge that a key to economic success is the ability to speak formal or Standard English. Therefore, a question that continues to surface is how to teach students to use formal or Standard English without devaluing the student's home language" (p. 6). The authors stress the importance of teachers accepting children's home language, while recognizing their responsibility to teach the formal English they will need to succeed in school and society. According to Van Keulen, Weddington, and DeBose (1998), respecting children's cultural and ethnic background and accepting their home language go hand in hand. Miller and Higgins emphasize that teachers should be careful not to use terms such as "standard" or "nonstandard" English, as they send the message that language is right or wrong. They further suggest for teachers not to directly correct a child's home language. If you think about where a child's home language comes from, you realize it comes from their family. If you correct their language or tell them they are wrong, you are telling them their whole family is wrong. Miller and Higgins talk about a situation in which one of the authors told a child he should not say "ain't." When the child responded with "What's wrong with 'ain't'? My daddy says it all the time," she decided she would no longer correct students directly, but she would find other ways to teach formal English (Miller & Higgins, 2006).

You can teach formal English through literature, which can serve as an excellent example of formal English and rich language (Tompkins, 2006; Wells, 1986). Students will emulate the formal language they hear read aloud. Miller and Higgins (2006) recommend reading the book *Don't Say Ain't* (Smalls, 2004) to show students an example of how they can use different language forms in different situations. The book is about an African-American child who goes to a new advanced school and meets her African-American teacher who uses very formal English. When she later hears her teacher talking to her godmother in her home language, she becomes confused. She learns that you use different language depending upon the different situations in which you find yourself. This book can serve as a springboard for a conversation about when to use formal English and when to use your home language. You can also have mini-lessons about when to use different forms of language, and you can serve as a model of formal English. I have often shared with my students that I might use the word "y'all" in everyday speech, but that when I am in a formal situation, I would not use that term. We talk about and role-play different situations when you might use formal English or home language. Researchers (Delpit, 1988; Goodman, 1965, 1973; Miller & Higgins, 2006) remind us not to directly correct children's home language, and Delpit (1988) emphasizes that minority children should be explicitly taught the language skills needed to participate in the dominant culture. We have that responsibility in order to help our students succeed.

Including Families

You can make your students feel accepted and valued by letting them know you want to learn more about their cultures. Inviting parents to come to the classroom to be a guest speaker is a great way to get families involved and celebrate the cultures of all children. Paley (1995) has invited parents from different cultures to come and tell stories about their lives and cultures to her Kindergartners. For example, a small African-American girl and her mother came dressed in clothes of African design to teach the class about Kwanzaa. They brought the kinara, colorful scarves, and other items used during Kwanzaa, as well as food traditionally served during Kwanzaa for the children to sample. The mother also read African folk tales to the children. Paley originally decided to invite the mother to speak on Kwanzaa when a former student, an African American, mentioned that she never had felt comfortable talking about Kwanzaa because none of her teachers ever mentioned it.

A Chinese mother came to visit our first grade classroom dressed in traditional clothing from China. She read a Chinese folktale, taught us a Chinese song, and showed us how to make spring rolls. The woman's daughter beamed with pride, as everyone watched intently. Another year, a second grade girl's mother came and read German folktales to us and passed out some German pastries. The little girl proudly wore a traditional German outfit her mom had made. All parents can be invited to share their cultures, share a special talent, teach the class words from their language, or read to the class. Parents should feel that they are a part of the community.

When you have a community of learners in which everyone feels comfortable sharing and celebrating their cultures, traditions, and languages, you have a group of students who will carry with them what they have learned about other people throughout their school careers and beyond. Students who are raised in a school setting that recognizes and celebrates diversity will grow into adults that have respect and appreciation for people who represent a wide variety of cultures, ethnicities, and languages.

References

Anders, R. (1976). *A look at prejudice and understanding.* Minneapolis, MN: Lerner.

Banks, J. A., & Banks, C. A. M. (Eds.). (1993). *Multicultural education: Issues and perspectives.* Boston, MA: Allyn & Bacon.

Beim, L., & Beim, J. (1947). *The swimming hole.* New York: Morrow.

Berg, H., & Miller, M. (2011, Spring). English language learners: Smoothing the transition. Texas Child Care.

Cherry, M. (2019). *Hair love.* New York: Penguin Random House.

Claire, E. (1994). *Where is Taro?* Orlando, FL: Harcourt Brace & Company.

Claire, E., & Haynes, J. (1994). *Classroom teacher's ESL survival kit #1.* Englewood Cliffs, NJ: Alemany Press/Prentice Hall Regents.

Cooper, D., & Kiger, N. (2008). *Literacy assessment: Helping teachers plan instruction.* Boston, MA: Houghton Mifflin Company.

Delpit, L. (1986). Skills and other dilemmas of a progressive black educator. *Harvard Educational Review, 56*(4), 379–385.

Delpit, L. (1988). The silenced dialogue: Power and pedagogy in educating other people's children. *Harvard Educational Review, 58*(3), 280–298.

Delpit, L. (1995). *Other people's children: Cultural conflict in the classroom.* New York: The New Press.

Derman-Sparks, L., & The A. B. C. Task Force (1989). *Anti-bias curriculum: Tools for empowering young children.* Washington, D. C.: National Association for the Education of Young Children.

Freire, P., & Macedo, D. (1987). *Literacy: Reading the word & the world.* South Hadley, MA: Bergin & Garvey.

Goodman, K. S. (1965). Dialect barriers to reading comprehension. *Elementary English, 42,* 853–860.

Goodman, K. S. (1973). Dialect barriers to reading comprehension revisited. *Reading Teacher, 27*(11), 6–12.

Goodman, K. S. (1986). *What's whole in whole language?* Portsmouth, NH: Heinemann.

Hale, J. E. (1982). *Black children: Their roots, culture, and learning styles.* Provo, UT: Brigham Young University Press.

Kuykendall, K. (1992). *From rage to hope: Strategies for reclaiming Black and Hispanic students.* Bloomington, IN: Solution Tree Press.

Levine, E. (1989). *I hate English!* New York: Scholastic.

Miller, M., & Higgins, B. (2006). When to say ain't. *Florida Reading Quarterly, 42*(4).

Motley, N. (2016). *Talk, read, talk, write* (2nd ed.). Irving, TX: Seidlitz Education.

Paley, V. (1979). *White teacher.* Cambridge, MA: Harvard University Press.

Paley, V. (1995). *Kwanzaa and me: A teacher's story.* Cambridge, MA: Harvard University Press.

Seidlitz, J. (2019). *Sheltered instruction in Texas: Second language acquisition methods for teachers of ELs.* Irving, TX: Seidlitz Education.

Seidlitz, J., & Perryman, B. (2011). *7 steps to a language-rich, interactive classroom: Research-based strategies for engaging all students.* Irving, TX: Seidlitz Education.

Seuss, Dr. (1961). *The sneetches.* New York: Random House.

Smalls, I. (2004). *Don't say ain't.* Watertown, MA: Charlesbridge Publishing.

Templeton, S., & Gehsmann, K. (2014). *Teaching reading and writing: The developmental approach.* Boston, MA: Pearson.

Tompkins, G. (2006). *Literacy for the 21st century: A balanced approach.* Upper Saddle River, NJ: Pearson.

Tompkins, G. (2014). *Literacy for the 21st century: A balanced approach.* Boston, MA: Pearson.

Van Keulen, J., Weddington, G., & DeBose, C. (1998). *Speech, language, learning, and the African American child.* Boston, MA: Allyn & Bacon.

Wells, G. (1986). *The meaning makers: Children learning and using language to learn.* Portsmouth, NJ: Heinemann.

Yashima, T. (1955). *Crow boy.* New York: Viking Press.

Zygmunt, E., & Clark, P. (2016). *Transforming teacher education for social justice.* New York: Teachers College Press.

CHAPTER 9

Assessing Reading and Writing

Mr. Rosen has just delivered a mini-lesson for his first grade class, and they have gone to their seats to start Reading Workshop. He calls Keely to come to the conference table for a reading conference. She has been reading Mrs. Wishy-Washy *(Cowley, 1980), and her teacher asks her to read it to him. Mr. Rosen does a running record while Keely reads, and then he jots down a note saying that her fluency is improving. He asks Keely to retell the story and makes another note that she retold the story with accuracy. After Keely decides she will make a puppet show of the book, Mr. Rosen sends her off to work on her book project, and gets up to walk around and check on other students. He observes John and Jorge as they are buddy reading a book, and he writes down some anecdotal records in his notebook. Then he goes over to where students are working in literacy centers and asks them how things are going. He jots down some more anecdotal records of his kid-watching, then he goes back to the conference table and calls Santana to come for a conference. She gathers up her book and excitedly hurries to the conference table to read to her teacher.*

Ongoing Informal Assessment

It is important to know where your students are in terms of their reading and writing development, what your students know, and what they are able to do, in order to know what they need instructionally. Clay (1993) puts it eloquently,

"When children enter school we need to observe what they know and can do, and build on that foundation, whether it is rich or meagre" (p. 6). Bear, Invernizzi, Templeton, and Johnston (2004) state that teachers should "Start with what students can do and track progress over time" and ". . .focus on what students' errors tell us about what they know" (p. 37). We must meet every child where they are and build upon their strengths. Instruction should be guided by assessment. Tompkins (2014) emphasizes, "By linking assessment and instruction, teachers improve students' learning and their teaching" (p. 72). Routman (2000) stresses that ". . .when learners are well served, assessment becomes a learning experience that supports and improves instruction" (p. 559). She goes on to say that the teacher becomes a learner as well and learns about students and the instruction they will need. You can think of it like a patient going to a doctor. The doctor has to diagnose the patient so they will know what medication or advice to give the patient. In teaching, the teacher has to assess the students in order to know what instruction they will need. It is helpful for the teacher to begin the year by finding out where each student is in terms of reading and writing development, then monitor their progress throughout the year through ongoing informal assessment.

Avery (2002) emphasizes the importance of remembering the following things about assessment when it comes to young children:

1. Look at development and growth—avoid a deficiency model.
2. Recognize that learning/growth patterns are uneven, recursive, and individual.
3. Examine the growth of the individual—avoid comparison of others.
4. Set goals—with students—but be flexible. Remember: growth may go in unpredictable directions; avoid measuring against predetermined standards.
5. Recognize the limitation of tests.
6. Include student self-evaluation.
7. Recognize *all* assessment procedures and tools have an element of subjectivity and bias—including my own methods. (p. 458).

The Observation Survey (Clay, 1993) is an excellent tool to give to emergent readers and writers to get a good picture of the child's literacy development. The assessment begins with letter ID, to determine which letters the child knows and can name. The teacher records whatever the child says, whether it is the letter name, the sound, or another letter altogether. Next, the teacher asks the child to write down all the words they know for the Word Test. If the child has trouble thinking of words to write, the teacher makes suggestions, such as "Can you write your name?" or "Do you know any color words?" This assessment is scored by words that are spelled correctly.

In the Observation Survey, students' concepts about print are also assessed. The teacher asks questions of the child about a book that is placed in front of them, such as "Where is the top of the page? Where do you start reading? And where do you go after that?" The child is also asked to show one letter, one word, a question mark, etc.

The next part of the survey is Hearing and Recording Sounds in Words, in which the teacher dictates a sentence to the child, and the child writes it. This part is scored by how many sounds the child could record, rather than by correct spelling.

The final part of the Observation Survey is the Reading Test. During this part, the child begins by reading a book on an easy level, then moves through higher levels as able. The teacher does a running record to check for accuracy of reading, then analyzes the miscues to see if they were using meaning (semantic), structural (syntactic), or visual (graphophonic) cues. The Observation Survey gives the teacher exact knowledge of what the child knows, so she is able to cater lessons to meet the needs of each and every child. In addition, the teacher keeps a running list of letters and words each child knows, as well as their current reading level.

Informal Reading Inventory

An Informal Reading Inventory (IRI) gives us a vivid picture of student reading development (Flynt & Cooter, 2003). There are many different commercially published IRIs that can be used, such as the Flynt Cooter Test (Flynt & Cooter, 2003) and the *Bader Reading and Language Inventory* (Bader & Pearce, 2015). IRIs typically include a word recognition list or placement sentences to show teachers where to start, and reading passages at graded levels.

In most IRIs, the student begins by reading the reading passage silently, then retells the story. The teacher may also ask additional comprehension questions that are included with the inventory. The student then reads the passage aloud, and the teacher records miscues, which will later be analyzed to determine strategy use (Cooper & Kiger, 2005). Typically, teachers will assess all students with an IRI at the beginning of the year, in the middle of the year, and again at the end of the year to determine students' progress. While the teacher is assessing each student with the inventory, other students can do reading and writing workshop or literacy centers.

IRIs determine the students' instructional reading level, as well as which cueing systems (semantic, syntactic, and graphophonic) students use. This information can help teachers place students in their guided reading groups with students who read on the same or similar levels. Knowing which cueing systems students use helps teachers plan mini-lessons, word work, and teaching points to work on during guided reading. If the teacher notices students are neglecting to use a certain cueing system, they can focus on strategies and prompts that will encourage the use of that cueing system. Remember, when students are reading books in guided reading, it is important that they read on the instructional level (books that can be read with 90% to 95% accuracy) so they will be able to practice the reading strategies they have learned as they work through the text (Clay, 1993). Between administration of IRIs, teacher can use running records to keep weekly progress of students' reading level, strategy use, and cueing system use.

Running Records

Clay (1993) states, "Running records capture what the readers said and did while reading books or texts. Having taken the record teachers can review what happened immediately, leading to a teaching decision on the spot, or at a later time as they plan for the next lessons" (p. 4). Running records are done by sitting next to the child as they are reading and making a check on a blank sheet of paper for accurate reading, or writing the word substituted for the word on the page (Fountas & Pinnell, 2017). The teacher also notes if a word was repeated by writing an "R" after the word. If a whole phrase is repeated, a line is drawn under the repeated text with an "R" at the end. Teachers also note if a word was inserted by writing it above a line and putting a dash under the line. If a word was omitted, the omitted word is written with a line and a dash over it. When the child asks for the word and the teachers tells the word, it is marked as "A/T." If the teacher gives the word without being asked, it is marked as simply "T." Here is how the markings look:

Accurate reading	√√√
Repetition	R
Substitution	house/home
Omission	-/home
Insertion	the/-
Teacher told	T
Student asks and teacher tells	A/T

Here is an example of a running record for a text that said, "The wolf blew the house down," and the child read, "A wolf blew the home down."

a/the √ √ √ home/house √

After the child has read, the teacher writes MSV beside each miscue. These initials stand for meaning, structure, and visual, and they represent which cueing systems the child was using when they made the miscue. The teacher circles the cueing systems used. For instance, if the child read "home" for "house," the teacher would circle "M," as the words have the same meaning. The teacher would also circle "S," because the miscue is also structurally correct. In fact, the child was also using visual cues because the words begin with the same letter and have two more letters that are the same, so the teacher would circle "V." This tells us that even though the child made a miscue, they were using all of their cueing systems. On the other hand, if a child read "bunny" for "rabbit," the teacher would circle just "M" and "S." Although the child was using meaning and structural cues, they were not using visual cues, since "rabbit" and "bunny" are not visually similar. The running record is so valuable because, not only does it record accuracy of reading, but it helps the teacher see what cueing systems the child is using. This enables the teacher to focus on teaching the child to use the other cueing systems as well, through a mini-lesson, a conference, or prompting.

Spelling Inventories

According to Bear et al. (2004), "Spelling inventories are words specifically chosen to represent a variety of spelling features or patterns at increasing levels of difficulty" (p. 34). The inventories include words that are representative of spelling features that correspond to the different stages of spelling, and they are an excellent way to learn about students' understanding of orthography. According to the authors, the three steps for spelling assessment are to "(a) selecting and administering a spelling inventory, (b) analyzing students' spelling, and (c) monitoring growth and planning instruction" (p. 36). Some teachers begin the inventory whole group, then continue only for students who have spelled most words correctly. The teacher calls out each word twice and reads the word in a sentence if students need context. The student writes each word on a blank sheet of paper or a numbered sheet of paper. Younger students may need access to an alphabet strip to remind them of how to form each letter. Students' spelling is analyzed by referring to the error and feature guides included in the spelling inventory. You will be able to determine your students' spelling stages through the inventory, and this will enable you to cater to mini-lessons, conferences, and literacy centers to meet their individual needs. The authors recommend administering a spelling inventory three times during a school year in order to best assess students' understanding and progress. Again, it is important to guide your instruction with assessment and monitor your students' progress.

Observations and Anecdotal Records

Once the teacher has done the initial assessments with each child, they can monitor children's progress by observing as they are reading and writing. This practice is referred to as "kid-watching" (Owocki & Goodman, 2002) because teachers watch students as they participate in literacy activities. Tompkins (2014) states that kid-watching involves carefully watching what students do as they are reading and writing. The author recommends planning kid-watching so that every child can be observed at least once a week.

The teacher typically makes a checklist to keep track of reading and writing behaviors, using literacy stages as a general guideline. On a checklist, teachers have a predetermined criteria, and students are aware of the criteria ahead of time (Tompkins, 2014). It is also helpful to take anecdotal records to record reading and writing behaviors seen, questions they ask, strategies they use, or statements they make (Gillet, Temple, & Crawford, 2004; Tompkins, 2014). It helps to write down the strategies and skills they use to determine what they may or may not be understanding and what needs to be taught in a future mini-lesson (Tompkins, 2014). For instance, a first grade teacher might write:

"9/18/19: Logan and Jared are partner reading *Dan, the Flying Man* (Cowley). Each reads a page at a time, and Logan helps Jared with the word 'bridge.' They are both reading fairly fluently." Or "10/5/19: Macy read "The cat is sot" for "The cat is soft." She went back and re-read and self-corrected. Macy points to the words as she reads. She is making more self-corrections than she did a couple of weeks ago."

The teacher can keep a notebook with checklists and anecdotal records. One idea is to record the observations on sticky notes, then transfer them to a notebook (Boyd-Batstone, 2004; Tompkins, 2014). Anecdotal records can also be taken during reading or writing conferences.

Rubrics

Rubrics are scoring guides teachers use to compare student work to specific criteria in order to make an evaluation on student progress (Tompkins, 2014). Rubrics communicate teachers' expectations to students (Templeton & Gehsmann, 2014).

For rubrics to be effective, students should have access to them as they are creating their literacy assignment. Many times, students self-assess using the rubrics and even create their own rubrics. According to Tompkins, creating rubrics for writing helps students learn to think about their thinking and about their writing.

6 + 1 Traits of Writing

As we discussed in Chapter 6, the 6 + 1 Traits of Writing is a scoring system students and teachers can use for writing. It was created in the 1980s by teachers who wanted to get a holistic look at students' writing that could tell them more than a single standardized test score. The Northwest Regional Educational Laboratory (NWREL) used these components as a writing assessment model and as a basis for descriptive criteria to describe good writing qualities. According to NWREL (2004), six key qualities define strong writing. The plus one refers to the presentation of the text on the page, for instance, a student might make book in the shape of a dinosaur. The following are the 6 + 1 Traits:

1. Ideas—the idea or purpose of the writing
2. Organization—the organization or structure of the writing
3. Voice—the writer's personal style
4. Word choice—the words used by the author to convey meaning and sound pleasing
5. Sentence fluency—the flow of the words and variety of sentences
6. Conventions—mechanical correctness of the writing

+1. Presentation—how the text looks

The 6 + 1 Traits are used with the writing curriculum as a tool for revision. Students learn through mini-lessons how to assess their writing using the 6 + 1 Traits and to make revisions based upon the traits. These traits provide the language needed to teach students what to revise, and they can learn how to use the traits through mini-lessons. 6 + 1 Traits fit naturally into the writing process as they make teaching writing more focused and purposeful.

Reading and Writing Conferences

During Reading and Writing Workshops, conferences are a great way to check in with students and see how they are doing. Tompkins (2014) describes reading and writing conferences as a time to have a conversation with students about their literacy and set goals together. According to Templeton and Gehsmann (2014), teachers can learn a lot about a child's literacy skills and their use of strategies through reading and writing conferences. In a reading conference, a teacher might take a running record, ask a child about the book they read, or have them retell a story. Routman (2000) suggests that teachers use reading conferences as an opportunity to assess comprehension and observe strategy use. In addition, the teacher can check in with the child to make sure they have chosen a book on their reading level. The reading conference is also a good time to encourage the child to think about how they felt about the book and decide what project they want to do to respond to what they have read.

In a writing conference, the child typically reads their piece to the teacher, and teacher and child talk about the piece together, make plans for the writing piece, or revise and edit. Routman (2005) encourages teachers to conference with students before, during, or after writing to respond to students by listening to their writing piece, determining confusions, teaching to those confusions, scaffolding, and helping them set goals for their writing. Fletcher and Portalupi (2001) tell us that even children whose writing is represented by drawings can participate in writing conferences. Teachers can encourage the child to write something to go along with their pictures or add to the pictures. Children can also be encouraged to say the words they want to write and listen to the sounds they hear in order to write down the letters or words. For students who are writing conventionally, the authors suggest asking them questions about parts of the piece that are unclear and encouraging them to think about what stands out as being the most important part or the theme and making sure to focus on that topic. Teachers can even show students how to cut and paste or tape their piece to add something new or rearrange their writing during the conference.

A conference is also a good time to give the child individual instruction on a skill or strategy. When taking notes during conferences, it is best to write down behaviors seen and avoid evaluative statements (Templeton & Gehsmann, 2014). A teacher can gain more useful information when specific behaviors are written down for them to go back and read later to make plans for instruction. Writing statements, such as "great job" will not give you as much information.

Work Samples

Work samples can be writing pieces, reports of science activities, reading projects, models, videos, photos, or any product that shows students' progress over time. Cooper and Kiger (2005) recommend examining work samples to determine what the student knows and what confusions they might have (Cooper & Kiger, 2005). Tompkins (2014) suggests that teachers monitor students' progress by collecting recordings of their oral reading, samples of their writing, and photos of projects they have made in response to their reading. Work samples are also excellent examples of student work to show growth over time and can be used in parent conferences.

Portfolios

Routman (2000) describes a portfolio as "a reflective selection of artifacts, work samples, and records that demonstrate who we are as literate beings (readers, writers, thinkers, and learners) and how we have developed over time" (p. 562). Students collect their writing pieces and choose special ones to go into their writing portfolio (Tompkins, 2014). They may choose pieces that they are especially proud of, pieces in which they tried something new, or pieces that show growth. Typically, teachers will encourage students to put the date on their work or stamp it with a date stamp so they can see how much they have grown as a writer over the year. Students write a reflection on their writing piece and explain why they chose that piece to go into the portfolio. A portfolio is also very nice to show parents during parent conference time to show how far their child has come from the beginning of the year. At the elementary school where I taught and my children went, they kept a portfolio that included work done from Kindergarten to fourth grade. It was an amazing collection of work that told the story of Marsh and Missy's literacy learning, and I cherish those portfolios to this day.

Self-Assessment

Portfolios help students begin to think about self-assessment of their literacy learning. Tompkins (2015) states, "Children learn to reflect on and assess their own reading and writing activities and their development as readers and writers" (p. 96). Children as young as 5 are able to self-assess when expectations and criteria are clear (Templeton & Gehsmann, 2014). The authors state, "Like any new tool or strategy, teaching students how to self-assess will require modeling, guided practice, and independent application with ongoing feedback" (p. 149). In self-assessment, students think about their likes and dislikes of reading material and how they see themselves as a reader. They also identify what they like about their writing piece, or what they might want to change, and how they have grown as a writer. Teachers and students can discuss the characteristics of good reading and writing through conferences and mini-lessons (Tompkins, 2015). Teachers might talk with students about "What fluent reading is, which reading strategies children use, how children demonstrate their comprehension, what makes a good project to apply reading knowledge, what makes an effective piece of writing, which writing strategies are most effective, how to use writing rubrics, and why correcting mechanical errors is a courtesy to readers" (p. 96).

According to Atwell (2007), students in the reading workshop are "in a constant state of evaluation" (p. 125). They are continuously choosing books, keeping reading logs, monitoring, making and presenting book projects and books talks, and setting goals. Atwell asks students to think about the various reading and writing activities they are involved in and asks them to reflect on questions such as, "What's something new that you tried as a reader, author-, genre-, or process-wise? How did it work out for you?" and "What's a book that took you by surprise this trimester?" (p. 127). She also asks them to complete the sentence stem: "I now realize the following about myself as a reader _____" (p. 127). When students use self-assessment, they think about their own thinking and about their reading and writing and begin to take responsibility for their own learning.

Parent Conferences

You can think of parent conferences as a time to showcase the progress your students have made. When students are having difficulty, it is best to address that difficulty with parents right away, instead of waiting for formal parent conference time. Even when you have to have a conference to address a struggle the child is having or a behavior challenge, it is good to start off the conference with something positive. Parents love to hear good things about their children, and they will be much more receptive to listening to something more negative after hearing the positive first. Also, remember to end on a positive note as well. If you have to address a challenge or a struggle, it is a good idea to make sure you and the parents leave the conference with a plan in mind.

Some schools choose a certain day on which parent conferences are scheduled all day long, and students are not in school. In one school where I taught, we had a waiting area with a couple of chairs outside our rooms with magazines so parents could wait comfortably if they arrived early. Teacher were instructed to wear the school T-shirt and khaki pants so they would all look the same and perhaps seem less intimidating to parents who were uncomfortable coming to the school. One teacher I know had a parent who could not come to parent conference day because she had to work driving a taxi, so the teacher called for a taxi and requested the parent. She asked to be driven to a fast food restaurant and ordered an iced tea for both the parent and herself, and they had the conference on the way.

In some schools they involve the students in the conferences, and they come to the school with their parents at the scheduled time. Students can have specific things to show their parents, such as their writing portfolio or work samples, and they can practice what they will say about their progress before the conference. Atwell (2007) describes how her students participate in student–parent–teacher conferences: "Every student also compiles a portfolio—three-ring binders that children fill with representative, captioned examples of their work across the disciplines—and presents it to parents and teacher in a student-led evaluation conference" (p. 127). This is a wonderful way for students, teachers, and parents to have a conversation celebrating the growth the child has made over the year. Of course, challenges can still be addressed, but that will be easier when the tone of the conference has been so positive.

High-Stakes Tests

High-stakes standardized tests are a reality in today's society. Unfortunately, when there is so much emphasis on high-stakes testing, many teachers may forego ongoing informal assessments that are so helpful in guiding instruction. According to

Campbell (2002), "Literacy assessment is first and foremost about student learning, yet issues of accountability consistently overshadow this basic principle" (p. 17). The test often becomes the focus and takes the place of authentic teaching and learning. Too many times, test prep activities become the primary instruction.

Though many teachers feel pressure from their administration and districts to teach to the test, Higgins, Miller, and Wegmann (2007) state, "High-quality, evidence-based instruction need not be sacrificed in preparing students to succeed on standardized writing assessments" (p. 310). Gallagher (2009) reminds us that "recreational reading actually is test preparation. When students read books recreationally they are building valuable knowledge capital that will help them in future reading" (p. 117). Fletcher and Portalupi (2001) tell us "Your students will perform fine on these tests so long as you provide them with regular opportunities for writing in the workshop" (p. 109). Tompkins (2015) emphasized "good writing instruction is the best way to prepare children for on-demand writing assessments" (p. 332). She stressed that children who use the writing process and 6 + 1 Traits of Writing to write to a variety of genres are successful writers. However, standardized writing tests further require children to understand what the writing prompt is asking them to write, and they have a limited amount of time to write during the test. Children are accustomed to choosing their own topics in Writing Workshop, but on a standardized writing test, they are asked to write to a prompt that they may have no interest in writing about. Tompkins advises teachers to ensure that children are ready for the writing test by teaching them to "analyze the prompt, develop ideas, plan their writing, and proofread" (p. 333). Fletcher and Portalupi (2001) remind us that when students write in the workshop, they are accustomed to rereading their writing pieces. They also develop an inner voice and anticipate questions a reader might ask of their writing piece. When students are writing in the workshop, you can encourage them to find and solve problems within their writing and reflect on what does and does not work for them and what strategies they use. All of these writing habits will help students as they write for a standardized test (Fetcher & Portalupi, 2001). Fletcher and Portalupi suggest that you provide students with practice on the testing format and coach them to use all they know about writing on the test. Tompkins (2015) recommends teachers interrupt Writing Workshop for about 6 weeks prior to testing time in order to learn and practice these testing strategies, as described in a study by Shelton and Fu (2004). Students using this process scored higher on the state test, though they disliked the test preparation. Tompkins states, these students "eagerly returned to Writing Workshop where they chose their own topics, collaborated with classmates and didn't have to adhere to time restrictions" (p. 333) when the testing was over. This is a good compromise to help students get ready for the writing test while still using best practices for overall writing instruction.

The important thing I want to leave you with is that your instruction should be guided by assessment. Always know your students, know what they know and can do, and use that information to find out what is best for each and every child. Make sure your instruction comes from your ongoing informal assessment and that high-stakes standardized assessments are seen as an interruption in the process, rather than the focus of instruction.

References

Atwell, N. (2007). *The reading zone: How to help kids become skilled, passionate, habitual, critical readers.* New York: Scholastic.

Avery, C. (2002). *. . . And with a light touch: Learning about reading, writing, and teaching with first graders.* Portsmouth, NH: Heinemann.

Bader, L., & Pearce, D. (2015). *Bader reading and language inventory.* (7th ed.) Upper Saddle River, NJ: Pearson-Prentice Hall.

Bear, D., Invernizzi, M., Templeton, S., & Johnston, F. (2004). *Words their way: Word study for phonics, vocabulary, and spelling instruction.* Upper Saddle River, NJ: Pearson Merrill Prentice Hall.

Boyd-Batstone, P. (2004). Focused anecdotal records assessment: A tool for standards-based, authentic assessment. *The Reading Teacher, 58,* 230–239.

Campbell, M. (2002). Constructing powerful voices: Starting points for policy driven literacy assessment reform. *Journal of Reading Education, 27,* 17–23.

Clay, M. (1993). *An observation survey of early literacy achievement.* Portsmouth, NH: Heinemann.

Cooper, J. (2000). *Literacy: Helping children construct meaning.* Boston, MA: Houghton Mifflin.

Cooper, J. D. & Kiger, N. D. (2005). *Literacy assessment: Helping teachers plan Instruction.* Boston: Houghton Mifflin.

Cooper, J., & Kiger, N. (2005). *Literacy: Helping children construct literacy.* Boston, MA: Houghton Mifflin.

Cowley, J. (1980). *Mrs. Wishy Washy.* New Zealand: Shortland Publications.

Cowley, J. (1980). *Mrs. Wishy-Washy.* Los Angeles: Hameray Publishing.

Fletcher, R., & Portalupi, J. (2001). *Writing workshop: The essential guide.* Portsmouth, NH: Heinemann.

Flynt, S., & Cooter, R., Jr. (2003). *Reading inventory for the classroom.* New York: Pearson.

Fountas, I., & Pinnell, G. (2017). *Guided reading: Responsive teaching across the grades.* Portsmouth, NH: Heinemann.

Gallagher, K. (2009). *Readicide: How schools are killing reading and what you can do about it.* Portland, ME: Stenhouse Publishers.

Gillet, J., Temple, C., & Crawford, A. (2004). *Understanding reading problems: Assessment and instruction.* New York: Pearson.

Higgins, B., Miller, M., & Wegmann, S. (2007). Teaching to the test…not!: Balancing best practice and testing requirements in writing. *The Reading Teacher, 60*(4).

Northwest Regional Educational Laboratory. (2004). 6 + 1 Trait writing—About. Retrieved August 2, 2006, from http://www.nwrel.org/assessment/about.php?ode

Owacki, G. & Goodman, Y. M. (2002). *Kidwatching: Documenting children's literacy development.* Portsmouth, NH: Heinemann.

Routman, R. (2000). *Conversations: Strategies for teaching, learning, and evaluating.* Portsmouth, NH: Heinemann.

Routman, R. (2005). *Writing essentials: Raising expectations and results while simplifying teaching.* Portsmouth, NH: Heinemann.

Shelton, N., & Fu, D. (2004). Creating space for teaching writing and for test preparation. *Language Arts, 82,* 120–128.

Templeton, S., & Gehsmann, K. (2014). *Teaching reading and writing: The developmental approach.* Boston, MA: Pearson.

Tompkins, G. (2014). *Literacy for the 21st Century: A balanced approach.* Boston, MA: Pearson.

Tompkins, G. (2015). *Literacy in the early grades: A successful start for PreK-4 readers and writers.* Boston, MA: Pearson.

CHAPTER 10

Loving School

Ms. Ling calls her first graders to the carpet for story time. As they take their places, she shows the cover of the book <u>The Very Lonely Firefly</u> (Carle, 1999), and asks the children, "Have you ever seen a firefly when you are outside in the evening?" Shelby says, "We saw some fireflies last night! They were pretty!" Camilla says, "My mommy calls them lightening bugs!" Jack excitedly jumps up and exclaims, "One time I saw fireflies, and we caught them in a jar, then we let them go!" "Well," says Ms. Ling, today we are going to read a very special book about a firefly that was lonely. It's called <u>The Very Lonely Firefly</u>, and it is written by Eric Carle. Why do you think this firefly is lonely?" Valentina says, "Maybe he can't find his friends!" Then Emelio offers, "Maybe he can't find his mommy!" Ms. Ling says, "Oh, could be! Those are both reasons he might be lonely. Let's read the book and find out." She starts to play a recording of "Swan Lake" by Tchaikovsky," and begins to read, as the children listen with wonder. When Ms. Ling finishes the story, she shows the children the last page of the book that has fireflies that light up. They respond with a chorus of "Ahhhh" and "Wow!" Next, Ms. Ling passes out small flashlights to several children and turns out the light. As "Swan Lake" continues to play, she asks them to turn them on and shine them on the ceiling, making the imaginary fireflies fly around. A few students clap their hands, as they all gaze toward the ceiling. Each child gets a turn to shine a flashlight, and many of them stand up and dance around gracefully when it is their turn. Others giggle with delight or say, "Ooh, pretty!" as they make the fireflies zip back and forth.

The scenario above paints a picture of wonder, fascination, and joy. As I look back over my days as an elementary school student and as an elementary school teacher, that is what I remember. I remember the excitement of every new day—what was to be learned that day, what we would read, what we would write, what we would create, and how we would sing and dance. I love school. I have always loved school. I love the smell of a new box of crayons and the feeling I had when I used a smooth, broken crayon to shade in a beautiful piece of artwork. I love the smell of paste and the way a pencil looks when it has just been sharpened. I love the feeling you get when a second grader bursts into the room and says, "What are we gonna read today?" I love the energy you feel when you walk into a classroom, hung with student work, that has the most amazing community of learners, who are eager to see what each new day holds for them. Each year, from the first day of school, I wanted the best experiences for each and every student. I wanted all students to feel intelligent, accepted, celebrated, safe, secure, loved, trusted, and appreciated for their differences and their sameness. It is important that children feel a sense of community from day one, and that they not only know your expectations from the moment they enter the classroom, but that they also know from the first moment that you care for them and are there to help them succeed. It is possible to make your classroom an exciting, enjoyable, comfortable, safe place for both the children and for yourself. In this final chapter, we will talk about some of the ways you can make that happen.

Creating a Community

In any classroom, it is beneficial to create a community of learners, in which every child feels included, safe, and respected. To create such a classroom, it is important for teachers to set and keep an atmosphere of mutual respect from the very first day by showing the children they trust and care for them. Teachers can show respect and care for students by taking time to get down to their level and really listen to what they are saying. This will help children understand how the teacher values them and is interested in what they say and think. Children will learn from the teacher's example and will show respect for the teacher and for classmates. They will feel like a team, and they will get the sense the teacher and students are "all in this together."

Creating a print-rich environment in the classroom is another way to build a feeling of community. It is important for students to be surrounded by the written word. Templeton and Gehsmann (2014) describe the print-rich classroom as "a classroom environment that is nearly saturated with print" (p. 75). The authors remind us that the classroom will evolve over time with "tracks of children's thinking" (p. 75) displayed throughout. Walls can be decorated with colorful posters with content or motivational sayings, anchor charts, students' work, and a word wall. Remember to make sure posters depict all ethnicities and abilities. In addition to the book center with a variety of books and cozy pillows, it is a great idea to have a writing center. The writing center can contain a variety of paper and things to write with, including pencils, markers, crayons, and chalk. Materials for publishing books should also be available, and everything should be easy for children to reach.

It is a good idea to provide seating that is conducive to group work. If you don't have tables, you can puts desks together in a cluster, so students are able to collaborate. Each table can contain a basket with supplies for the group, such as scissors, markers, crayons, and pencils, and a bin of familiar books for individuals or for the table group. I always used to have an individual alphabet strip and a name tag for each child in their workspace.

It is also a good idea to have a central place for children to meet with the teacher for whole group instruction. Many teachers provide a large carpet for students to sit on or individual carpet squares. I always had a rocking chair at the front of the whole group area, a whiteboard, and an easel for big books. During DEAR time, students could sit in the rocking chair to read. I made sure to include lamps to make the lighting softer and play soft music, as I always wanted our classroom to be cozy and comfortable. The classroom atmosphere can help create a feeling of inclusion and community.

All students, and especially ELs, should have plenty of time to talk every day. I always used to tell my class that I should hear a busy hum as they were working. If it got too loud, I would give my signal by raising my hand and saying "signals up." Then I would pretend to turn the volume down. It is important for students to have conversations with each other to process what they are learning through both structured conversations (QSSSA) and casual conversations. Children learn language by using it, so a classroom should be a noisy place!

One teacher I know displays children's work underneath their photograph with their names printed on a sentence strip. This helps the children to feel valued and to feel ownership over the classroom. Another teacher has a bulletin board that has a cutout of a tree. All of the children have a name tag in the shape of an apple, and they place the apple on the tree with Velcro when they arrive each day. When children are absent, their name tags are placed on a cutout of a heart, and the children sing (to the tune of "Farmer in the Dell") "We'll keep you in our hearts, we'll keep you in our hearts, Sarah, Lionel, and Shante, we'll keep you in our hearts." When children return, they know they were missed. Creating a nurturing environment and a feel of community helps students feel comfortable and secure each day when they come to school. For many children, school is the place they feel the safest and the happiest.

It is essential for children to know what is expected of them at all times. Modeling, role-playing, and practicing procedures help children understand and internalize classroom expectations. It is important to take the time to explain things in a way that children can understand. Classroom rules or standards can be introduced using literature, such as *David Goes to School* (Shannon, 1999). Another good way to help the children feel ownership over the classroom is to let them help set the rules or standards. It is also good to talk to them about why it is important to have and follow rules (so we will know what to do, so no one will get hurt, etc.). Children feel empowered when they help set the rules, and they are also more likely to follow the rules if they understand why we have certain rules, and why it is important to follow them.

Classroom rules can have this type of language: "Clean up any mess you make" and "Be kind to one another," rather than "No talking," "No running," etc. to create a kinder, gentler feel. Warner and Lynch (2004) remind us to use positive language and be aware of our facial expressions when we enforce expectations. It is also important to remember to be consistent in how you deal with behavior issues that come up. The authors suggest trying to prevent challenges by giving students reminders of procedures before an activity. Warner and Lynch also suggest praising good behavior and ignoring negative behavior when possible, unless someone is getting hurt. When a child must be corrected, it is best to do it quietly and in private, so as not to embarrass the child. Remember to "address the behavior, not the child," (p. 39), and if you forget and accidentally yell at a child, apologize.

In *Wally's Stories*, Paley (1981) describes how her Kindergarten children took turns dictating and acting out stories that dealt with classroom behavior, rules, fairness, and social issues. This practice served as a springboard for conversation about how members of the classroom community should treat and act toward each other. In this type of discussion, students can be encouraged to come up with solutions to behavioral challenges that might arise.

Focusing on the Positive

To keep your attitude positive, Warner and Lynch (2004) suggest "emotional getaways" (p. 27), such as reading a good uplifting book, going for a long walk, calling or visiting an old friend, watching your favorite movie, or treating yourself to a new outfit. You can also talk to your class about positive attitudes and discuss what it means to have a positive attitude. Students can role-play different situations and what a positive attitude looks like in each situation. It is also important to make positive phone calls home. When Missy was in third grade, her teacher called to welcome her to the school year and tell her how excited she was to have her in class. We had gone out to dinner to celebrate the beginning of the school year, and when we got home her teacher had left a message on the answering machine. Missy was so excited that her teacher had called, and she listened to the message over and over!

A sense of humor will go a long way toward helping you focus on a positive attitude. It is fun to laugh with the children and enjoy every day you have with them. You only have them for 1 year (in most cases), and this is your chance to try and make it their best year of school that they will recall fondly in the years to come. Use music, do Readers Theater frequently, and have puppet shows. Find out about the children's families, their sports, musical or dance activities, and what they are interested in. One boy I taught in second grade had been sort of a challenge. He invited me to his basketball game, and I went with my husband. After that, we had such a connection, and he was very well behaved. I also remember how proud I was when my husband said the child was very athletic!

Inviting parents into the classroom as often as possible will help build community and make each child feel valued. Parents can come and read to the class, share a special food or talent, talk about family traditions, or teach students a game. In one school where I taught, we had an open-door policy and encouraged parents to come whenever they wanted to and as often as they wanted. They could come and have lunch with their child or bring a family pet to share, or help in the classroom. I had one parent that came and read individually with each first grader in my class. I went to both Marsh and Missy's classrooms to read once a week on my conference period, as they always went to the school where I taught. The same children were always in class together, because our school had family groups, and I can remember watching them grow from Kindergartners to fourth graders and seeing how big they looked sitting together on the carpet as the years passed.

It is also fun to find out about students' pets and tell stories of your own pets. Even when Marsh was in seventh grade, he had a teacher who told stories about her dog every day. He came home every afternoon with stories about his teacher's dog. I remember one day, he came home and said the dog had minty fresh breath because she had eaten a tube of toothpaste!

It is important to learn students' names quickly at the beginning of the year and always call them by name. It is always fun to play name games at the beginning of the year so you and the students can all learn and use each other's names. When each child enters each morning, remember to greet them and say their name. You may be the first person who has been pleasant to them that morning. At one school where I taught, teachers were supposed to stand by their door and hug each child as they came in each morning. Many teachers give students a choice of a hug, a handshake, or a high five every morning. One teacher was recently on YouTube showing how each child had their own personal greeting between themselves and their teacher whenever they came in the room. Students need to know we are happy to see them every day. It is especially important to acknowledge and celebrate each child's birthday, even those in the summer. In the elementary school where I taught and my children attended, the principal let children come to the office to say their name and age on the microphone on their birthday during morning announcements. When it was their birthday, my students and Marsh and Missy were always excited to talk on the microphone, and they looked forward to it all year!

It also helps you to stay positive when you look for humor in situations and jot down cute and funny things the children say. For example, one year, I was teaching a class of 3-year-olds, and we had some gerbils in an aquarium. Two little boys would always say, "Hey, let's go say, 'you tick' to the gerbils!" Then they would go to the gerbils and say "you tick" over and over to them while pointing at them. I was quite perplexed by this ritual until I realized they had seen me point to the gerbils one day and say, "You stink!" I have told this story over and over to students, family members, and friends. It is so much better to bring home humorous stories, instead of dwelling on frustrations. The public needs to hear us say positive things about our students and our schools. When we hear teachers talking negatively, we need to remember to stay away! Or even better, change the subject to tell a funny story from your classroom!

Using Music in the Classroom

Another way to build community and keep the environment positive is to use music in the classroom, which is natural and enjoyable for young children and teachers alike. Teachers who integrate music into their classrooms provide "a nurturing environment for young readers, writers, musicians, poets, actors, and dancers" (Miller, 2005, p. 38).

Combining Literature and Music According to Lamme (1990), teachers can make books come alive for students by using music along with literature. Miller (2005) gives the example of reading *Blueberries for Sal* (McCloskey, 1948), then singing "The Bear Went Over the Mountain" and "Teddy Bear, Teddy Bear, Turn Around." The author suggests having students bring teddy bears from home to act out the book and songs, then having a picnic with Teddy Bears, while listening to the song, "Teddy Bear Picnic" and reading *Teddy Bear's Picnic* (Kennedy, 2000).

Many books are made from children's songs. For example, *Today is Monday* (Baum, 1992), *Over in the Meadow* (Keats, 1971), *Frog Went a-Courtin'* (Langstaff, 1955), and *Fiddle-I-Fee* (Sweet, 1992) are songs written in the form of a book that Miller (2005) recommends. Marsh and Missy and my children at school all loved reading and singing *Today is Monday*. The version I have is a book that folds out, and the children have all loved unfolding it as they sing about the days of the week and different foods. Children's songs written as big books are perfect, as children are able to see the print while they sing. Two children I tutor, Carmen and her brother Isaac love to sing the big book, *Five Little Ducks* (Paparone, 2005). We use a mamma duck puppet and five baby duck finger puppets to act out the song. We have a "quacker" in the shape of a duck beak that sounds like a duck, and the children like to take turns blowing it when the mamma duck quacks. They ask to sing this book almost every time I work with them. They also take it home and read it to their parents and little sister. "Singing these books together promotes reading as the children's eyes are drawn to the printed lyrics," according to Miller (p. 38). Gipe (2002) states, "Wholesome musical lyrics from audio recordings can also support literacy, especially for learners whose learning styles are attuned to musical ways of representing meaning" (p. 61). You can find, songs, poems, and finger plays to go along with just about any book you can think of!

Using Rhythm and Rhythmical Books There are "many children's books that lend themselves to rhythmical activities because of their rhythm, repetition, and beat," according to Miller (2005). Children can make their own rhythm instruments by filling plastic Easter eggs with rice or by putting jingle bells on a pipe cleaner, and my husband made some rhythm sticks for my classroom with dowel rods. I love reading *Chicka Chicka Boom Boom* (Martin & Archambault, 1989) while the students play along on rhythm instruments! *Crocodile Beat* (Jorgensen, 1989), poems, and predictable books are also good to read in this way. According to McCracken and McCracken (1986), "Poetry is meant to be heard. Its rhythm and cadences and rhyme, if any, make it a natural vehicle for introducing children to print" (p. 102). The authors explain that nursery rhymes contain "all the cadences of spoken English in short stanzas, enticing children to chant them over and over" (p. 102). Hopkins (1987) refers to poetry as "word music," and Norton (1995) states, "poetry often has a musical quality that attracts children and appeals to their emotions" (p. 392).

Background Music Miller (2005) states, "Classical music used as background music sets the mood for the classroom and inspires children as they read and write" (p. 39). According to Gipe (2002), "Played as soft background music, the sonatas, etudes, concertos, and symphonies add an ambience of peacefulness, unity, and creativity" to the classroom (p. 371). Music can also provide background for oral reading, Readers Theater, and poetry reading. Polette (1989) tells us, "When the reader uses music as a background for oral reading, the words flow from the page with expression and feeling. It is a good way to get beyond the mere words of a passage to the images and emotions that underlie the selection" (p. 56). Maurice Sendak used to listen to music by Wagner as he wrote children's books (Norton, 1995), and children can listen to the same music as they listen to *Where the Wild Things Are* (Sendak, 1963) and create puppets or masks. I did this in my second grade classroom, and we danced with our puppets to "The Ride of the Valkyries" by Wagner, then we watched the opera version of *Where the Wild Things Are* (Sendak, 1963).

Painter (1989) tells us, "there is absolutely nothing more practical and magical than music to back up and enhance your storytelling to children" (p. 1). In my class, I read *Goodnight Moon* (Brown, 1947) with "Nocturne No. 2 In E-Flat Major" by Chopin as background music, and I read *The Very Busy Spider* (Carle, 1984) with a creepy, crawly spider puppet while a jazzy version of "The Itsy Bitsy Spider" by Thomas Moore played in the background.

You can also use music as a signal for transitions. You can greet children with a song each morning, while using their names by singing "Let's sing hello to Landon, Let's sing hello to Sydney, etc.," or you can sing a certain song when it is time to go home. My Kindergarten teacher always sang to us, "Good-bye, now, good-bye now. The clock says it's time! I'll see you on Wednesday, good-bye, now, everyone." It was such a fond memory, that I also sang it to my students each afternoon. I remember my nursery school teacher singing, "It's time to put the toys away, toys away, toys away. It's time to put the toys away so we can play tomorrow." Again, I sang the same song with my classes, as I always thought it was so special when my teacher sang that.

Music can also help the class refocus. You can stand up and sing and do the motions to "The Hokey Pokey" for a stretch break, or you can play "Stars and Stripes Forever" and have the students march around the room with rhythm instruments. You could pass out scarves or streamers and have the children dance to Tchaikovsky's "Swan Lake." Little bodies were not meant to sit still for long periods of time, and everyone will be more happy and comfortable after activity. "A classroom in which music and language arts are integrated nurtures children as they become readers, writers, and musicians," states Miller (2005, p. 40).

Combining Art and Literature

Teachers can include art in their language arts classrooms by studying the illustrations of picture books they are reading and finding out what medium the illustrator used. Students can emulate the pictures in the books or make a completely original picture using the same medium as the artist.

It is also a good idea to invite local artists come to visit the class to talk about their artwork. My sister, Sondra Schwetman, is an art professor at Humboldt State University. When she was in town for a gallery opening one week, she came to my second grade class to talk to them about the artwork she does and to invite them to her gallery opening. She then played classical music and had them make some artwork for us to hang around the room. Those pieces stayed up all year, and many students used some of the techniques she talked about in the illustrations of the books they made. Several students even came to her gallery opening!

Another idea I got from Sondra is to make a Joseph Cornell box about children's favorite books. This is a box with a scene from the book or something that represents the book with things they find around the house, around the classroom, or outside. Students create the box with the found art to show how they feel about the book. They love making something similar to artwork done by a famous artist!

Slowing Down

In the age of standardized testing and state standards that need to be met, it is easy to speed through each day trying to get as much done as possible. When this happens, children sometimes learn a little bit of everything and not much of any particular topic. Rather than get as much done as possible, try to get as much out of every day as possible. Rather than skating over the top of the curriculum, try to slow down and learn the content in depth. Give children time to ask questions, explore, and investigate. In addition, science and social studies sometimes get left out in favor of test preparation, and music and art are usually the first to go. As we have talked about in this chapter, it is beneficial to students to include both art and music, and to make them a part of language arts time.

Science and social studies can also be combined with language arts, using reading and writing as tools to explore the content. In one school where I taught, the first grade team had a collection of big books on science topics we shared and rotated each week. We combined picture books and informational text with the big books as we passed them along, and students were encouraged to read the books and write about the science topics. For instance, we had a big book about the different kinds of bears. Each time we read about a new kind of bear, students made a page in their own little bear-shaped book with information on the type of bear, where they are found, and facts about the bear. They read bear stories and nonfiction books about bears.

Finding Magic in the Classroom

As a Kindergarten, first, and second grade teacher, I can remember the wonderful experiences that my students had during reading workshop. They would read books of their choice for a designated amount of time each day, have a conference with me about their books, and come up with elaborate writing pieces and puppet shows, plays, dioramas, and book jackets as they responded to what they had read. My students were so excited about their reading projects, they often asked to go share them with the class next door or with the librarian. That was magic to me.

One year, I had a second grade child who could read and write fluently in both Spanish and English. She asked if she could read a book to the class in Spanish, and we borrowed a big book from the bilingual teacher, and she read it to the class in Spanish. Her eyes sparkled with pride as she read, and the class and I were mesmerized. That was magic to me.

During writing workshop, they would choose topics and take their papers through the writing process to develop beautifully illustrated published pieces. They excitedly shared their writing pieces with parents, grandparents, siblings, and teachers at Young Authors Day. They always eagerly planned their next writing piece after publishing each one. We wrote class books based upon predictable books we had read. For example, we wrote a class book called, *A House is a House,* based upon the book, *A House is a House for Me* (Hoberman, 1978). Each student made a page on which they completed the sentence stem "A _____ is a house for a _____," and illustrated it. We laminated it and read it over and over. That was magic to me.

In my first grade class, we sang songs every morning, and some of the students spontaneously got up and danced during our songs. Our morning song time quickly turned into our morning song and dance time. When we did a study of bears for a couple of weeks, students brought their own teddy bears to school, sang songs about bears and danced with their teddy bears during song and dance time. After treating their bears to a Teddy Bear Picnic with cupcakes, Teddy Grams, and juice boxes, the study culminated with a teddy bear factory. Children brought paper bags from home and scraps of cloth, buttons, lace ric rac, and feathers, and each one created their own teddy bear. At the end of the study, they were so excited to take their masterpieces home! That was magic to me.

In one of my second grade classes, we had a boy named Bobby who had Cerebral Palsy. The first day of school, he came into the classroom in a wheelchair. Three boys immediately ran to him and said, "Can I push your wheelchair?" They all four began to laugh at the same time and became the best of friends right from the first day of school. The boys took turns being Bobby's scribe when it was writing time, and they actually fought over whose turn it was. He always told the most elaborate stories. One in particular was about a tall goose who lived in a tall shed. Throughout the year, all the children in class played with Bobby and wanted to help him in any way possible. When students from other classes would stare at Bobby, my children would say, "Don't stare at him! He's our friend!" A mother of one of my students said that her daughter had seen someone park in a handicapped parking spot that did not look to be disabled. She said to her mom with tears in her eyes, "What if Bobby's mom needed to park there?" Bobby eventually got to the point that he was walking with crutches instead of a wheelchair. When he came to school for the first time with his new crutches, all the children cheered, and some of them cried. I cried also. That was magic to me.

I hope you will find magic like my students and I did. Your magic may come in a different way than ours did, but one thing's for sure—it will not come in the form of test prep, writing prompts, or reading passages. I hope you find a school where test prep is not the practice, and where you can teach to your own passion. Or, perhaps, you will find a school where you can be the change agent and help everyone understand the value of authentic meaningful reading and writing experiences, as opposed to the scripted lessons that are rearing their ugly heads in some schools today.

Every child deserves to be in a place where they feel safe, and they feel a sense of belonging. All children should see themselves in the literature and on the walls of the classroom. All children should receive the message that they are valued, their families are valued, and their culture is valued. They all deserve to find magic as they learn to read, write, listen, speak, dance, act, sing, and create poetry. All children should hear the message loud and clear that they can do great things, and that it begins right here, in this classroom. I hope you find something in this book that inspires you to live your best teaching life and make magic happen for yourself and your students. May you be an inspiration to all the children, parents and teachers, whose lives you touch.

References

Banks, J. A., & Banks, C. A. M. (Eds.). (1993). *Multicultural education: Issues and perspectives.* Boston, MA: Allyn & Bacon.

Baum, S. (1992). *Today is Monday.* Singapore: HarperCollins Publishers.

Bierhorst, J. (1979). *A cry from the earth: Music of the North American Indians.* New York: Four Winds Press.

Brown, M. (1947). *Goodnight moon.* New York: HarperCollins.

Carle, E. (1984). *The very busy spider.* New York: Penguin.

Carle, E. (1999). *The very lonely firefly.* New York: Penguin.

Cornett, C. E. (2003). *Creating meaning through literature and the arts: An integration resource for classroom teachers.* Upper Saddle River, NJ: Merrill/Prentice Hall.

Derman-Sparks, L., & the A. B. C Task Force (1989). *Anti-bias curriculum: Tools for empowering young children.* Washington, D C: National Association for the Education of Young Children.

Gipe, J. P. (2002). *Multiple paths to literacy: Classroom techniques for struggling readers* (5th ed.). Upper Saddle River, NJ: Merill/Prentice Hall.

Hoberman, M. A. (1978). *A house is a house for me.* New York: Penguin Books.

Hopkins, L. B. (1987). *Click, rumble, roar: Poems about machines.* New York: HarperCollins Juvenile Books.

Jorgensen, G. (1989). *Crocodile beat.* New York: Simon & Schuster Children's Publishing.

Keats, E. J. (1971). *Over in the meadow.* New York: Scholastic.

Kennedy, J. (2000). *The teddy bears' picnic.* New York: Aladdin Books.

Lamme, L. L. (1990). Exploring the world of music through picture books. *Reading Teacher, 44*(4), 294--300.

Langstaff, J. (1955). *Frog went a-courtin'.* New York: Scholastic.

Martin, Jr., B., & Archambault, J. (1988). *Listen to the rain.* New York: Simon & Schuster.

Martin, Jr., B., & Archambault, J. (1989). *Chicka chicka boom boom.* New York: Simon & Schuster.

McCloskey, R. (1948). *Blueberries for Sal.* New York: Viking.

McCracken, R. A., & McCracken, M. J. (1986). *Stories, songs, and poetry to teach reading and writing: Language through literacy.* Chicago, IL: American Library Association.

Miller, M. (2005). We can sing a rainbow: Using music in the language arts classroom. *The Florida Reading Quarterly, 41*(4).

Norton, D. E. (1995). *Through the eyes of a child.* Englewood Cliffs, NJ: Prentice Hall.

Painter, W. M. (1989). *Musical story hours: Using music with storytelling and puppetry.* Hamden, CT: Library Professional Publications.

Paley, V. (1987). *Wally's stories: Conversations in the kindergarten.* Cambridge, MA: Harvard University Press.

Paparone, P. (1997). *Five little ducks.* New York: North South Books.

Polette, N. (1989). *Reading with music.* St. Louis, MO: Gateway Publishing.

Sendak, M. (1963). *Where the wild things are.* New York: HarperCollins.

Shannon, D. (1999). *David goes to school.* New York: Scholastic.

Smardo, F. (1984). Using children's literature as a prelude or finale to music experiences with young children. *The Reading Teacher.*

Sweet, M. (1992). *Fiddle-i-Fee: A farmyard song for the very young.* New York: Scholastic.

Templeton, S., & Gehsmann, K. (2014). *Teaching reading and writing: The developmental approach.* Boston, MA: Pearson.

Tompkins, G. E. (2005). *Language arts: Patterns of practice.* Upper Saddle River, NJ: Merrill/Prentice Hall.

Ungerer, T. (1958). *Crictor.* New York: HarperCollins.

Warner, L. (1982). Thirty-seven music ideas for the non-musical teacher. *Childhood Education, 58.*

Warner, L., & Lynch, S. (2004). *Preschool classroom management: 150 teacher-tested techniques.* Beltsville, MD: Gryphon House, Inc.